Who Is Agent X?
Proving Science & Logic Show It's More Rational To Think God Exists

Neil Mammen

D1534052

Rational Free Press

Who is Agent X? Proving Science & Logic Show It's More Rational to Think God Exists

Edition 8.7 unreleased
Copyright © 2009, 2010, 2011, 2012 by Neil Mammen

Edited by Richard W. Stevens
legalriter@gmail.com

Email the author at AgentX@NoBlindFaith.com
All rights reserved.

Published in the United States by
Rational Free Press
1165 Lincoln Ave, #8321
San Jose, CA 95155-8321

Cover Photo: The Helix Nebula, NGC 7293, also anthropomorphically called "The Eye of God." Visible light image compiled from the Hubble Telescope and ground-based images in 2004. Credit: NASA, ESA.

Other titles by this author:
Jesus W̶A̶S̶ IS involved in Politics! Why aren't You? Why isn't Your Church? Rational Free Press, 2010.
40 Days Towards a More Godly Nation, Rational Free Press, 2012
Who is Agent X? The Slides, Rational Free Press, 2013
Quantity copies of this book maybe also be ordered at large discounts.
To order these or other books go to
www.JesusIsInvolvedInPolitics.com

To my gorgeous wife Anna
and
the little girl
Mary-Katherine
who changed my life
by making me understand a little of why
a Non-Mechanistic
Extra-Dimensional
Free-Willed
Personal
Agent
would so much want a loving relationship
with someone who is
helpless,
occasionally defiant
and who doesn't even comprehend Him

To sweet Caroline Lois Mammen
my daughter who is enjoying a multi-dimensional
existence with God today
and has left a legacy of life for my friends
by creating an opportunity for them to hear
the "Apologia" for our Hope

Special Thanks to Richard Stevens for editing this revision

Richard was a wonder. He spent months editing; cleaning, researching quotes and having me clarify things so he could rephrase key concepts.
I cannot thank you enough Richard.

CONTENTS

Introduction:
A Challenge

Dear Reader,

Chances are that a friend has given you this book to evaluate its contents and decide if the claims we make here are sound. In light of that, please consider this book a friendly challenge.

No Blind Faith is a small team of scientists, teachers, and engineers, who subscribe to the thinking that all blind faith is *not only* dangerous but could also be evil. We hope that you share this conviction with us, especially if you are an atheist.

Our goal in this series of books is to use scientific, historical, and archeological facts to present our cases. We will **not** use the Bible, religious doctrine or anyone's blind or superstitious beliefs as proofs. We refer to any of these only when evaluating their accuracy, rationality, and cohesiveness, or to discuss their relevance philosophically.

In this particular book by Neil Mammen, we intend to use only scientifically accepted facts to evaluate if it is logically more rational and reasonable to believe that a personal first cause of the Universe exists.

Over the years, numerous friendly and not so friendly[1] atheists who have reviewed this book have come up with many seemingly valid objections. Indeed, as you read this, you may think of numerous objections yourself. We recognize that, and rather than try to cover every potential objection *within* the text itself, which would make for dry reading, we've gathered as many objections as we've been given and included them and their responses in **Appendix I: Objections.** This way we can give these important objections their due consideration. So, may we recommend you also read this Objection Appendix in its entirety before concluding that you have an objection we've missed?

If you do indeed come up with an objection that no one has come up with before, or one that is not a combination of already answered objections, we would be happy to hear and respond to that

---

[1] Okay, some have been downright belligerent, we are not sure why, because we are all very nice people.

objection. We might include our response to it in future editions of this book. Similarly, if you find a fact that we've either accidentally misinterpreted or gotten wrong (and we're sure there are a few), we want to immediately correct them for future revisions. It only hurts us if we have made errors; it is not our intention to be duplicitous or wrong.

Send any corrections to **Xobjections@NoBlindFaith.com.**

Visit **www.NoBlindFaith.com/AgentX.htm** for a live list of these updated corrections and objections.

To the Christian Reader:
One of our goals at No Blind Faith is to enable you to engage with co-workers and friends with this perhaps daunting material without getting in "trouble" and without your friends starting to feel that you are an evangelizing pest. Thus, we urge you to read **Appendix III: Using this Information without Fear** after you have finished with the main text.

Happy Thinking
The Team at No Blind Faith.

...religion without science is blind...
Albert Einstein, Ideas and Opinions (1954)

www.NoBlindFaith.com

Chapter 1:
A Rational and Logical Case

I'd like to present a rational and logical case for how I came to my conclusions about the first cause of the Universe. I don't want you to feel that I am forcing my views on you, but having said that, I do want to emphasize that what I am going to present is *not* an opinion or a belief. It's an ***argument***.

While I agree that it's very hard to prove a negative (see the footnote for evidence that it's not *impossible* to prove a negative[2]), I want to state up front that if any atheist could indeed prove to me that it is more reasonable to believe that God does *not* exist, I will immediately stop being a theist. I can think of better things to do with my time, energy and money.

In return, please consider this offer: if I am able to show it is indeed more reasonable to think that God does exist; and if I can do that using science and logic, without appealing to any religious authority; then would you seriously consider the further claims of Christ? Surely, that's fair.

I'm not asking you to become a believer in Christ at this point, just to investigate His claims further. After all, if the person who gave you this book, or I, am really right, you could be going to

---

[2] If anyone says "It's impossible to prove a negative!" ask him if that is a negative statement (it is because it claims it's *not* possible to do something). If it is a negative statement, how can he prove that statement itself? Moreover, the assertion is simply not true. Here's a negative statement that you can prove easily: "There are no prime integers between 7 and 9." That negative statement is easily provable by looking at the integer 8 which can be divided by 4 and 2 and thus is not a prime number and is the only integer between 7 and 9. So some negatives are indeed provable.

Hell[3] and surely, that's worth some of your time and energy to investigate. I'm not saying that the mere *possibility* of Hell necessarily means you should get "fire insurance," but rather it's worthwhile to *investigate* if you should. If someone tells you that a bridge is out, surely it behooves you at least to exercise caution and check it out. Well, the person who gave you this book and I think the bridge *is* indeed out.

I could be wrong. Of course I don't think I am, but I could be.[4] However, if you remember your Freshman Logic 101 courses, you will remember that there are only two ways to refute an argument.

You have to either:

(a) Show the facts[5] are wrong or incomplete; or

(b) Show that the logic is wrong.

There is no other way to refute an argument.

So, if you think my argument is wrong, that's how you will need to refute it. Note too: if both the facts and the logic are correct, then the motivations or the desires of the presenter of the argument become irrelevant. At that point, it matters not *why* I believe what I believe, but only if my argument is sound. So even if you think I am biased (which I am of course - but so are you), you cannot use "bias" to discredit my argument if you cannot show (a) or (b) above.

This is room 12A, Arguments, not room 12, Abuse[6]

In the years that I've been discussing this particular topic, I must say I've received more ad hominem attacks, i.e., atheists being rude and calling me names, than I have received actual valid objections. I'm not complaining; I expect this sort of flak. But even Monty Python knew that such abuse is not argument. Abusing someone is not a valid rebuttal.

---

[3] We'll discuss "where" Hell may be in chapter 5.

[4] Of course, if you disagree with me then you think I'm wrong and you think you are right. So apparently, it's okay to think you are right and others are wrong. I include this point because I've run into a few folks who *disagreed* with me, saying that we shouldn't disagree with each other. Go figure. To see more illogical statements like this refuted, go to www.NoBlindFaith.com/sermon/sermons.htm and click on "Suicide Statements."

[5] Remember, the facts have to be relevantly and significantly incorrect. Unless a seemingly minor error is shown to be significant, the error may not change the logical conclusion.

[6] Monty Python's Flying Circus, Episode 29, The Argument Clinic Skit, 1972. Recall they said, "An argument is a connected series of statements to establish a definite proposition." Also, "Argument is an intellectual process. Contradiction is just the automatic gainsaying of anything the other person says."

In addition, telling someone "well that's just your opinion," "I disagree with your approach," or even "we'll never know" (very popular amongst agnostics), is also not a valid rebuttal. You see, I'm presenting an argument; disparaging or minimizing the arguments without a point-by-point refutation does not work. They have to do (**a**) or (**b**) above. In fact, those who engage in abuse or any other types of disparaging comments, may be indicating that they do not have a valid rebuttal and have been forced to these alternate means (and it also indicates they are in the wrong room).

Still, aside from asking you to seriously consider what we present please do not feel that the person who gave you this book or I want to force our views on you at any time. I like to consider myself a rational person, and this is the logic behind my views and perhaps the views of the person who gave you this book to critique. We want you to evaluate it. Maybe it will help. Maybe it won't. You don't need to make an immediate decision though; mull on it for a while.

Don't reject the logic

Also please remember: **Do not let the consequences of your logic force you to reject that logic.**

I've often found people who reject reasoning, not because the reasoning is faulty, but because they don't want the consequences to be true. We see this every day as denial. A man rejects that he has cancer, because of what that may mean about him dying. A battered wife rejects that her husband is evil and won't change, because of what that means about her marriage and herself. Similarly, alcoholics or gambling addicts reject their addiction status because it implies weakness in themselves.

As you read, ask yourself: could you be rejecting this logic because of what the implications are? Moral implications, social implications, lifestyle implications, "submission to a supreme authority" implications? Could you be rejecting the consequences of your logic because it would mean you were wrong and have been wrong (even shouting your errors at the top of your voice)?

The best way to deal with any issue is to face the facts and try to deal with the truth, however ugly that truth maybe. So in the same way, don't let the consequences of the logic I am about to present you force you to reject it. See if the logic is sound, and then deal with the consequences independently, whatever they are.

In other words, I'm asking that you think rationally and not emotionally. If a God really exists, then we have to deal with the consequence of that separately. Can we agree that only irrational people will abandon the truth or the reasonableness of the existence of something, just because they don't like the fact that it will change their perception of reality? Or because it would have moral consequences?

Abandoning "God"

I'd like to abandon the word "God" for most of this discussion of the concept of a first cause. I do this because I don't want to presume that the first cause of the Universe is God.

We will postulate that some unknown *agent* caused the Universe; I'd like to call this cause Agent X. (The letter X is the traditional symbol for something unknown in math and science.) Agent X is the first cause. It could be a piece of hyperspace, it could be a yet undiscovered particle of physics, it could even be a photon, or it could be an alien as some suggest and of course, it could be nothing. We will try to approach it rationally and try not to force fit our desires onto it. As such, we will start by postulating that God is separate from Agent X.

A quick note to the Kantians

Some of you readers, rather than being atheists, may follow instead the theory that Immanuel Kant proposed, i.e., that mankind can never prove the existence of God. In fact, in discussing this topic, I've had folks who are normally very logical in their thinking, immediately say, "Oh, but you can't merge science and faith. That isn't possible." When I ask "Why?" they don't know. "Isn't it obvious?" they ask. It actually isn't.

To readers who feel this way, let me ask you for a favor. Remember Kant never proved that his theory was right. He just said, "I can't do it, so you can't either." Yet, it is reasonable that if God existed and He *wanted* us to discover Him using science, then He could make that possible, right? Of course, He could. He could show up in the sky and point at us. Or He could do amazing miracles, or He could if He wished put evidence throughout Creation that pointed to him. These possible options alone prove Kant was wrong.

So here's the favor: In this book, I'll present a logical and rational *scientific* proof that God exists. Then when that is done I want you to look at both sides. One side is a detailed rational proof of the existence of God. The other side is Kant's statement, "You can't use science to prove God exists." No proof, no logic, just Kant's statement. As a logical thinking person, which one should hold more weight for you?

Imagine if this were a murder case. The prosecutor says, "Ladies and gentlemen of the Jury, here's the evidence. The defendant owned this gun; forensic data shows that the barrel markings match the bullet that killed the victim. The defendant has no alibi, the defendant owed the victim lots of money, the defendant swore he'd kill the victim, the defendant has been imprisoned for violence and attempted murder before, and the defendant was seen leaving the victim's house the night after the murder when shouting was heard by the neighbors."

Then the defense attorney stands up and just makes a statement with no argument and no proof, "The defendant would never be able to kill anyone because *he* said so. The defense rests." Then he sits down. Do you want an argument like that to set a violent murderer loose in your neighborhood?

Kant made a claim, I present an argument. Kant provided no proof, I provide proof. You decide. How do you live your life? Do you buy a used car with no evidence of its reliability? Do you buy a house without a home inspection?

Maybe Kant is wrong? On the other hand, *I* could be wrong. Perhaps I can ask that you keep an open mind about that, as we look at the evidence.

Four Points

In this book, we are going to focus on these four main points:

(1) The Universe had a beginning.
(2) The Universe is fine-tuned.
(3) The Universe has more than four dimensions.
(4) The Earth seems to have been placed in a precise location designed for easy scientific discovery of the Big Bang and Cosmology.

We will state the evidence for them and use them to derive the characteristics of Agent X, whatever or whoever it is, if it *is* any *thing* at all, of course.

Now, let us examine the need for an Agent X and the characteristics of Agent X.

Chapter 2:
The Big Bang

To start we have to do a quick review of the history of science and scientists' understanding of the Universe.

Past History

About 80 years ago, atheists including most atheistic scientists said:

1. Everything that has a beginning has *a* cause[7], and anything that *existed forever* needs *no* cause.
2. The Universe had no beginning and existed forever.
3. Therefore, the Universe needs no cause (no causal agent, i.e., no Agent X).

In other words, they said that because the Universe has always been around, asking where it came "from" or asking what was "before" the Universe made no sense. This is a completely logical and valid explanation. This makes perfect sense if you think it through: If something has existed forever, it never did *not* exist. So it *need* not have a cause, because to have a cause, something has to precede it temporally (in time) or causally (cause-ally, i.e, in cause). Nothing could temporally (in time) precede anything that had existed forever.[8]

---

[7] When I say *cause*, I'm referring to Aristotle's *efficient* cause, see Objection 51 in the Appendix for an elaboration and explanation of this.

[8] Note that there is the philosophical possibility that an eternal object may have an eternal atemporal (non-time bound) cause, i.e., a cause that happened simultaneously. So it could causally but not temporally precede what it caused. I've not been able to come up with a valid example of this. Hume uses the example of a cushion with a ball on it that have both existed forever. Thus the dent in the cushion is caused by the ball, but both have existed

At the same time, theists and theistic scientists said:

1. Everything that has a beginning has a cause, and anything that existed forever needs no cause. (This is exactly the same as what the atheists said).
2. *God* had no beginning and existed forever.
3. Therefore, *God* needs no cause (or since God needs no Agent X as a first cause, God *is* Agent X).

This resulted in everyone being at a standstill. The Christians would ask: Where did the Universe come from? The atheists would respond: It's always been there, it doesn't need to come from anywhere.

Then the atheists would ask: Where did God come from? And the theists would say: He's always been there; He doesn't need to come from anywhere.

But, do note that one thing *both* atheists and theists agreed on was:

Everything that has a beginning must have a cause, and anything that existed forever needs no cause.

Repulsed by a beginning?

Remember too, that in those days, the atheists who were scientists were repulsed by the Christian concept that the Universe had *not* existed forever. Why? Because if the Universe had not existed forever, then it would need a cause. And they did not like the idea of it needing a cause. They were *counting* heavily on the fact that a Universe that had existed forever needed no cause. If you, dear reader, are an atheist, may I ask that you decide if you agree with the atheists like Bertrand Russell and numerous other scientists including Fred Hoyle? Do you agree with them that **if** the Universe existed forever, then it would need no cause? Let me repeat that

---

forever. Yet, it seems to me that any example using physical matter fails because there is no atemporal physical matter that we know of. Matter has electrons, and electrons have spin which need time. And as we'll see shortly, that was one of the lessons of the Big Bang i.e., matter can't exist without time. In eternity past there was no time. So I personally think Hume's example does not work. And I've not seen any examples of atemporal causality that *do* work so far, except for the Big Bang (it was caused atemporally outside of time) and ofcourse abstract concepts like 1+1 = 2. The addition of 1+1 caused 2. But 2 has also existed forever. So then I must ask, is 2 really caused by 1? This also is an example of how to ponder the Trinity? Did the Father precede (in time) the Son or the Sprit? We say He didn't but we do say the Spirit proceeds from the Father and the Son causally but not temporally. Just like the number 2. Fun stuff!

question. Answer for yourself: Do you agree that if the Universe *had* existed forever, it would need no cause?

Of course, you are hesitant to make a stance, for you think I am pushing you into a corner. You realize that if you say "no" you will be disagreeing with most scientists and will be holding an irrational and illogical position. But if you say "yes," you are worried that it will lead to a conclusion you don't like. But the reality is that it *is* a valid and true conclusion. To disagree would be illogical, unless you can rationally argue that my argument here, which is also Russell's argument, is false or illogical. You really won't be able to escape this issue.

It's important that you establish your response to this fact before moving on. So here's the question again: If the Universe had existed forever, would it be valid to say that it had no cause, that nothing could exist before it, that nothing could precede it causally and that it couldn't come from anywhere? In fact, can we agree that if the Universe had existed forever, then asking where it came *from* would be a rather unreasonable or ignorant question? Similarly, if the Universe had existed forever, asking what was *before* the Universe would also be a rather meaningless question.

If someone wishes to argue the very unscientific and unreasonable concept that not everything that has a beginning needs a cause, please refer to the Objections Appendix.

Recently we realized our Universe did have a beginning.

Some years ago, Hubble (the man, not the telescope) realized that some galaxies were redder than they should have been.[9] As scientists studied this phenomenon further, they realized that these galaxies were redder because the stars were traveling at incredible speeds away from us. This effect is called the Doppler Shift.[10] A simple example of the Doppler Shift is the sound a car makes as it passes us when we are standing by the side of a freeway. The sound of the car to us is higher in pitch as the car approaches us and lower in pitch as it passes. That's because although the sound the car is making is always the same, as the car moves towards us the speed of the car adds to the frequency of the sound and makes it sound higher. Why? Because each subsequent set of two waves are

---

[9] How did they know that they were redder? For an easy layman's explanation, see Simon Singh, *Big Bang: The Origin of the Universe*, (New York: Fourth Estate, 2005).
[10] Austrian physicist Johann Christian Doppler (1803–1853).

closer together than the last set. So the faster the car comes towards us, the more waves per second we sense. Once the car starts moving away from us, the frequency of the sound we hear is lowered as each subsequent set of sound waves hit us further apart from the last set. Then we sense fewer waves per second.

This same effect happens with the movement of stars. Red is a lower frequency of light. Therefore, as the stars rapidly move away from us, their light shining back at us looks redder/lower in frequency than it really is. We then look in other directions around us and we see the same thing. We see many galaxies are rapidly moving away from us (or that space is being created between us). If on the other hand we were to see a galaxy that is bluer than it should be, we'd better get out of the way fast – it is coming toward us.

I'm just kidding; it would probably miss us by a few million light years, but interestingly some galaxies are indeed coming towards us and will eventually collide with our Milky Way galaxy.

The first scientific conclusion: the Universe is expanding.

This conclusion causes some real problems.

First, if the Universe is expanding, that means it is expanding from something smaller. That means at some point it was very small and didn't exist. Therefore, it can't be infinitely old. Because if the Universe is expanding and is infinitely old, it would have long since expanded and all we'd see is white or gray light out there. I know you'd think we'd see nothingness out there, because everything would be infinitely far away from us. But it's possible that after an infinite time period, all that light would eventually reach the Earth and all we'd see is a gray light all around, but nothing would be close to us – nothing.

Since we can see that the Universe is still expanding, we can work backwards and calculate the point at which it started expanding. Stephen Hawking and most scientists agree that calculating backwards, we find the Universe, light, matter and everything suddenly came into being with a Big Bang about 13.7 billion years ago.[11] This was the point at which **matter** and **time** started to exist.

---

[11] The Big Bang marks the instant at which the Universe began, when space and time came into existence and all the matter in the cosmos started to expand. Amazingly, theorists have deduced the history of the Universe dating back to just 10^{-43} seconds (10 million trillion trillion trillion*ths* of a second) after the Big Bang.

This is an important statement. 13.7 billion[12] years ago, there was no time, there was no space. There was just a Singularity.

The state of the Universe just before the Big Bang is called the Singularity.[13]

A singularity is a point in space-time at which gravitational forces cause matter to have infinite density and infinitesimal (infinitely small) volume, and it causes space and time to become infinitely distorted. Prior to the Singularity, time, space, and other dimensions did not exist. The Singularity is thus the beginning of all known and measurable things.

---

[12] Some folks have asked if the 13.7B year timeframe means that the Bible is incorrect when it discusses a 6-day creation cycle. While there is insufficient space to discuss this here, this is a family argument amongst Christians (and also Jews). There are numerous valid **translations** of Genesis 1 and the word yom that allow for a longer creation time, note this is a question of *translation*, not *interpretation*. See Hugh Ross, A Matter of Days: Resolving a Creation Controversy, (Colorado Springs, CO: NavPress, 2004) and Rodney Whitefield, *Reading Genesis One*, (2003) www.AnswersInCreation.org (accessed November 25, 2012). Many times we interpret the Bible incorrectly based on our preconceived notions that aren't Biblical – for instance, following Plato's lead, the Catholic Church interpreted the Bible to indicate that the Earth was the center of the Solar System. Yet once Copernicus used science to prove it wasn't, we realized that there were actually no statements in the Bible that insisted that the world had to be the center of the Solar System. In addition, long before science even came up with the concept of time having a beginning, Augustine, Aquinas, Origen and many others in the first few centuries of Christianity all claimed that the word *yom* in Genesis could be translated as eon and (yes, thus literarily interpreted as eon and) not a 24 hour day. In other words, science seems to have adjusted itself to early Christian thinking, not vice versa. While this book does not argue the age of the Earth with atheists, this book does *not* take a hard and fast position on the age of the Earth, except to use what scientists have discovered and deduced. We use the data accepted by atheists to prove that God exists. Once they are saved one can argue Biblical hermeneutics and interpretation methods.
[13] www.pbs.org/wnet/hawking/universes/html/bang.html
"We showed that if general relativity is correct, any reasonable model of the Universe must start with a singularity...." Stephen Hawking, *Black Holes and Baby Universes and Other Essays*, (New York: Bantam Books, 1994).
A singularity is the point when a black hole collapses into itself and nothing can escape it once inside the event horizon, because its gravity is infinitely strong. It is a point where all matter is crushed into infinite density and space and time cease to exist, as we know it. The event horizon is the gravity field of a black hole. In this area space-time is so bent that light cannot escape it. The event horizon creates a region in space where nothing can escape because nothing can go faster than the speed of light. When something enters the event horizon, it therefore vanishes without a trace. If the object is emitting something, after it enters the event horizon, not even the emissions that traced its existence will escape the black hole. Time presumably stands still at the horizon. Does it reverse inside the black hole? Probably not, as we'd end up with a paradox, we really just don't know.

Then the Big Bang happens. And the Big Bang caused a lot of problems. The first problem scientifically and philosophically is: the Big Bang proves the Universe had a beginning. Remember what the scientists said: If something always existed, it needed no beginning. Well, the Universe didn't exist forever, so in this case it **does** need a beginning.[14]

Interestingly most atheistic scientists recognized this and for the first few decades after this discovery, they "abandoned the logic because of the consequences." The folks who proposed and presented papers on the Big Bang Theory were mocked, drummed out of universities, refused grants and were not allowed to publish their papers in peer review journals (this was not very scientific or rational of "my" scientific community, I'm embarrassed to say).[15] In fact, the very name "Big Bang" was a derisive name given to it by the scientist Fred Hoyle who was mocking the theory.

Atheistic scientists have said versions of the following:

Philosophically, the notion of a beginning of the present order of Nature is repugnant to me ... I should like to find a genuine loophole.
Arthur Eddington[16]

Remember this point for later, because many atheists now try to argue that things that have a beginning may need *no* cause. Yet the distinguished scientists quoted above would have ridiculed that idea. After all, why cause a big stink and make statements like the

---

[14] Note that scientists have tried to come up with a cyclical model, but it doesn't work. They are claiming the Universe collapses, then expands, and then collapses and so on. But so far, there is little to no proof of that, because if this were happening there would be residual energy left after each cycle and we do not see this. In fact, one could argue that if we did see this, it would still show us that the Universe is not infinitely old because after an infinity of these cycles, the entropy would be 100% and there'd be no useable energy left. In other words, if there was residual energy waste, it would show that the Universe is not infinitely old. One could however accept the cyclical model on "faith." Note too this comment *"It is said that an argument is what convinces reasonable men and a proof is what it takes to convince even an unreasonable man. With the proof now in place, cosmologists can no longer hide behind the possibility of a past-eternal universe. There is no escape, they have to face the problem of a cosmic beginning.* (Alexander S. Vilenkin, Many Worlds in One [New York: Hill and Wang, 2006], p.176).

[15] This is very reminiscent of the problem any scientist has today when they propose the concept of the need for an intelligent designer, which is an argument this book shows is not only valid but as we will see is more reasonable than the alternative.

[16] Arthur S. Eddington, "The End of the World: from the Standpoint of Mathematical Physics," *Nature*, 127 (1931): 447-53, 450, doi:10.1038/127447a0 (accessed November 25, 2012). p. 450

above quote about looking for a loophole, if you could just say, "Oh, everything popped into being out of nothing."

So today, science, logic and reason still tell us that:

1. Everything that has a beginning needs *a* cause; but anything that existed forever needs *no* cause.
2. The Universe *has* a beginning and hasn't existed forever.
3. Therefore, the Universe *needs* a cause.

Note when I use the word "cause" here, I'm talking about the primary cause, not an intermediate cause. For instance if you kick a ball that bounces off a wall and breaks a window. The wall maybe the intermediate cause, but you are the primary cause. That's the cause that concerns us.

Yet, since we don't know what this primary cause is, and we don't want to jump to the "God" conclusion, we will simply call this primary cause "Agent X."

Thus, the Universe needs an Agent X.

Agent X caused the Universe.

Agent X is the *primary* cause of the Universe.

Our job is to find out what or…

Who is Agent X!

To being with, we do know two things about this Agent X, don't we? Let's list these as we deduce them.

Philosophers tell us that since something cannot come from nothing, and since things exist, at least one eternal primary causer must exist. And being eternal it would need no cause. Note that while our Universe could have been caused by something that had a cause, if we go back all the way to the primary cause we realize that this causal agent itself existed before Time existed, so it is eternal and has no cause.

So we know:

1. *Agent X is eternal and exists forever*
2. *Agent X needs no cause.*

Chapter 3:
Causes and Mechanistic Agents

Now, some of my atheist friends have said: "Okay that's all fine. But this 'causer' Agent X, is just a small area of hyperspace that gave rise to the Singularity."

Other atheists have said: "We can use wave theory to prove that Agent X is just a mindless object, not existing in time and space. This object existed forever and the Universe has a 98% probability of arising."

In other words, they are saying, "Okay, we grant you that the Universe had a beginning, but what *gave rise* to the Universe had no beginning." They just push the problem back.

The need for a non-mechanistic agent

But that doesn't logically work. You see:
1. We know that the Universe has a beginning and a cause.
2. We also know that this cause (Agent X) cannot be mechanistic (i.e., it cannot be automatic – I'll explain this point in this chapter).
3. Thus, the cause must be a being that can *volitionally* decide to do something different.

Mechanistic Agent?

This is very important: The first cause needs to be a **non**-mechanistic agent. What is a *mechanistic* agent? I'm glad you asked. A mechanistic agent is something that does something once or a finite number of times, or does the same things over and over again and cannot change its mind or decide to do something different for no apparent reason, it's like a machine. It's mindlessly mechanical.

A **non**-mechanistic agent on the other hand is an agent that has free will, **can** change its mind and **can** decide to do something different.

A Mechanistic Agent would not result in a single Universe that was only 13.7B years old

Let me elaborate. Imagine if you had a top that was spinning. Does the top have a free will?

No, it is mechanistic, it's like a machine. In other words, it can't suddenly decide to start or stop spinning on its own free will, because it has *no* free will. If it's going to stop spinning, it will. If it's going to keep spinning, it will. But it can't up and change its *mind* and do something different.

With a mechanistic[17] top as the cause (the Agent X) of the Universe we'd only have two options. **Option 1**: the top would make universes on a repetitive basis. For example, every time the top made a complete revolution a universe is spawned; or **Option 2**: the top would only make one universe, for example when the top **stopped** spinning a single universe is spawned.[18]

Let's take **Option 1: Every time the top made a complete revolution, a universe is spawned.**

In this section I will use the word "infinite" for convenience. To be technically accurate we could use the phrase "as the number of events tend towards infinity" or "after gazillion to the power gazillion events," but those phrases are a bit bulky. So I'll just use "almost infinite" or "infinite" and you'll get the picture.

Okay, after an infinite number of opportunities arising in eternity past, how many universes would there be?

An infinite number of universes.

What about if the top spun around very slowly? Well, even if it takes a very, very long "time" to spin, after infinite "time"[19] or infinite causal events, how many universes would there be? Infinite! Why? Because as slow as the top spins, infinity is always much longer. Even if each spin takes a different amount of "time," or requires a larger number of causal events, it still ends up being infinite universes. But you ask what if the top takes infinitely long or eternity to make one spin? Well then, the Universe would *never* have been spawned, so this wouldn't help you at all.

---

[17] Note even a computer is totally mechanistic once you remove the program that was programmed by a being with free will. In fact, you could argue that even with a one-time program after eternity, anything that program was going to do would have already occurred in infinity past. Either way, you could never arrive at 13.7B years ago.

[18] If you try to argue that the top could have started spinning again, you'd end up back at Option 1 above.

[19] Note that I use the word "time" here to explain the concept, but in reality we are really discussing atemporal sequential causality (meaning events that take place outside of time, but with a cause-and-effect linkage). See the Appendix of Objections where we deal with the issue of how you can indeed discuss infinite causal events if there is no "time."

So Option 1 means we'd have to have infinite or an extremely large number of universes. This is confirmed even by the atheistic religion-hating astrophysicist Lawrence Krauss.[20] I note he's atheistic so atheists can't claim he's biased in my favor.

Consider **Option 2: When the top stopped spinning, a universe was spawned.**

In this case, if the top were going to stop spinning, there would be only one universe. But, if we looked back in eternity, how long ago would the top have stopped spinning?

Well, it stopped an eternity ago (i.e., the Universe would be eternally old). Why? Because however long it took for the top to spin down, eternity and infinity would be much greater and that would have passed *after* the top had stopped spinning.[21]

But our Universe is not infinitely old. It's only 13.7B years old.

Another example: The Eternal Alarm Clock

Let me present another example, in case the first was confusing. Remember, we are trying to show that only an agent with a mind could have created a single or finite set of universes 13.7 billion years ago.

Imagine that an alarm clock existed for all eternity. It just happened to be one of those high-tech alarm clocks that could "get" programmed in any complex set of ways. For instance, it could be programmed to ring once on a particular day, or it could be programmed to ring every day at a certain time, or it could be programmed to ring at 5 pm in 5 years (and then again at 6 am in 203 years, and so on). Or it could be **never** programmed at all.

Now, if there is no God and since the clock has existed for all eternity, it also had to have been programmed from all eternity. Why? Because there was no one around to program it, so either it has always been programmed or it has never been programmed. (Later we will deal with its being randomly programmed.)

---

[20] http://www.youtube.com/watch?v=0ZiXC8Yh4T0 at the 1:02:21 mark. Other questions he raises (earlier in the talk) like why such a big universe was made for puny humans are dealt with in the Appendix. Sometimes this video gets removed for copyright reasons. If so, do a search for "Krauss Dawkins '09: A Universe From Nothing"

[21] Note this option is also covered if the top is going to start and stop spinning *n* times. Why? Because if *n* is not equal to infinity then *n* will have ended eternally ago.

Therefore, the question is: Assume the alarm was programmed to only ring once, after a 100 years from its existence, at 3 am. After eternity, how long ago would the alarm have rung? Obviously: an eternity ago. There is no way it could have rung 13.7B years ago. What if it had been programmed to ring once after a 1 trillion years from its existence at 3 am. After eternity, how long ago would it have rung? Well again, *eternity ago* because eternity would be much much greater than 1 trillion. Note this also works if it was programmed to ring 1M times at different moments, all those 1M events would have occurred an eternity ago, none would have occurred 13.7B years ago.

Consider a second option. What if the program on the alarm clock was set to ring on a regular basis, e.g., every 3 billion years at 8 am or even every 2 trillion years at 4 am *and* 6 pm? Now fast forward to infinity. After infinite years, how many times will the alarm have rung? After eternity the clock will have rung infinite times, because however long the period we'd set the clock to ring at, as long as it was less than infinity, there would be an infinite amount of those periods in eternity past.

So now, imagine that the clock was some sort of unknown mindless Agent X; and instead of ringing an alarm, it would create a universe. We see immediately that we have only two options with an Agent X that has no free will. Either you get one universe that is infinitely old or you get infinite universes. There's no possibility to get only one universe 13.7B years ago.

Let's deal with the "randomly programmed" possibility. Let's say the alarm clock was accidently programmed to ring *once* by some random chance. That still wouldn't help because even if that chance was one in a gazillion, after eternity it would have been programmed infinite times.

Why is this so important?

Let me explain. You see if the first cause is a mechanistic agent like hyperspace or a lepton or some sort of extra-dimensional particle, then the logical conclusion is that our Universe would have been caused in eternity past or there would have to be an infinite number of universes. Why? Because the mechanistic agent can *only* do something once or it can do the same thing over and over again. Remember it cannot think, it has no free will, it has no mind to make a *decision*.

William Lane Craig explains this as follows:

In fact, I think that it can be plausibly argued that the cause of the Universe must be a personal Creator. For how else could a temporal effect arise from an eternal cause? If the cause were simply a mechanically operating set of necessary and sufficient conditions existing from eternity, then why would not the effect also exist from eternity?

For example, if the cause of water's being frozen is the temperature's being below zero degrees, then if the temperature were below zero degrees from eternity, then any water present would be frozen from eternity.

The only way to have an eternal cause but a temporal effect would seem to be if the cause is a personal agent who freely chooses to create an effect in time. For example, a man sitting from eternity may will to stand up; hence, a temporal effect may arise from an eternally existing agent. Indeed, the agent may will from eternity to create a temporal effect, so that no change in the agent need be conceived.

Thus, we are brought not merely to the first cause of the Universe, but to its personal Creator.

www.leaderu.com/truth/3truth11.html

Two Options

So to summarize, if a mechanistic agent had created the Universe, we'd have two options:

1. There would be an infinite number of universes; or
2. It would have created the Universe in eternity past. This means the Universe would be infinitely old.[22]

But, the Universe is only 13.7B years old and *not* eternally old; it was *not* caused in eternity past. So, something must have changed for it to occur. That change can only be a non-mechanistic agent that has volition or free will (meaning it can decide to do something different than it has been doing).

So, if the top had a free will and a mind and could one day 13.7B years ago think, "I will do something different 'now' than I have ever done 'before.'" [23] Then the top could stop spinning. In the same

---

[22] Even if the agent were going to create more than one, or any finite number of universes, all these universes would have been created in the infinite causal past. You may object that time did not exist at this point. We deal with this in some detail in the Objections Appendix.

[23] Of course, we are limited by language here because the free will agent looks like it knows the concept of time before time existed. Note here I speak of before in causal

way: If the Universe has not always existed, it would take a non-mechanistic being, i.e., a "Free Agent" with a will, to say: "Today/now/at this point,[24] I will create a Universe where and when there wasn't one before." And when it happened, it wouldn't have been an eternity ago but only 13.7B years ago.[25]

So to answer the initial objections:
Objection 1: Hyperspace created the Singularity.

The theory here is that an eternally existing piece of hyperspace is the cause of the Universe. But hyperspace is a mechanistic agent and has no free will, and we have seen rationally and logically this cannot be the solution.

Objection 2: The Singularity had a 98% chance of coming about spontaneously.

In that case it would have occurred eternally ago or infinite times. Because if something has a 98% chance of occurring, it will occur over and over again in infinity. Or it would have happened once eternally ago. But as we can see, the Universe is not eternally old nor is there proof of infinite universes (we'll discuss this in detail next).

Objection 3: Okay, we grant you that the Universe had a beginning, but whatever *gave rise* to it had no beginning.

And we all actually agree with this, but this simply pushes the problem back and doesn't solve it if you are trying to get a non-mechanistic first cause. We are trying to determine the necessary characteristics of what gave rise to the Universe and we realize that as much as you push it backwards, at some point, you are stuck with the

---

(that's cause-al not cas-ual) relationship not temporal relationship. In reality, the word "now" has no meaning at the Singularity. But a free will agent who is not constrained by time or space would be able to do "something." Note that you can have causal relationships without temporal relationships as Kant (whom I disagree with occasionally) explains with a ball sitting on a cushion from all eternity. The dent in the cushion is caused by the ball and the ball is raised because of the cushion for all eternity, so there's a causal relationship but no temporal relationship. Note we are not talking about the electrons in the cushion and the ball, but the cause of the dent by the ball.

[24] Whatever *that* means in a timeless eternity. In the objections appendix we discuss what if this meant all events occurred concurrently.

[25] In fact, one could even argue that perhaps if *any one thing* exists at all that is *not* eternally old, we need a non-mechanistic agent, but this is a philosophical argument that we will not address in any great detail.

need for at least one non-mechanistic free will primary agent.[26] And that primary Agent is what or whom we are interested in.

What about Infinite Universes?

At this point you may be thinking that I've missed the fact that the Universe could have *indeed* been created by a mechanistic agent that is constantly creating new universes[27] (also known as a multiverse or quantum universes, I call them the Infiniverse). Let me address this.

First, the moment you suggest that infinite universes are the solution to the issue of a non-mechanistic first cause, you have conceded a very important point. You've agreed that anything that exists forever needs no cause. You see, atheists and atheistic scientists propose this solution only because they believe that unless you have something that existed forever (like the cause of the multiverse or the very first universe of a multiverse) you need a first cause and that too, a non-mechanistic first cause. So beware of going down this path, as you will remove any objection to things popping up "out of nowhere" as a viable option for you (of course you could say, "Well it's just another option, but why offer it up?" Both are dealt with in the Appendix).

Still, how do *we* respond to the possibility of an infinite multiverse? Well, for one, there is **no** current evidence for infinite universes.[28] We cannot verify or refute them either. So one would have to take the multiverse idea on blind faith.[29] I always ask my atheistic friends if they really want to base their entire belief system on blind faith. If so, then I'd bet my rational faith (which this book presents) against their blind faith any day. I then ask, what is the difference between that theory of an Infiniverse and a myth of say the Great Serpent Spirit? Neither can be proven. The great atheistic solution is mythologically equivalent.

---

[26] By the way remember this objection, because my experience is that when atheists realize that they are in trouble they'll come back and claim that nothing had no beginning or things with beginnings need no cause.

[27] And this is what we'd expect to see if the "98% probable wave theory" was the cause.

[28] Paul Davies at one point postulated that the first universe created a bud universe that breaks off from its parent universe and that bud universe expanded and created another bud universe and so on and so forth. Note that Paul Davies now actually agrees that it's most likely that a God exists.

[29] We'll show how Loop Quantum Cosmology does not solve this problem in the Appendix.

My atheist friends are always telling me that if we can't measure, see, touch, taste, smell, hear, interact or verify close to 100% that something exists, (like God) then you are being a superstitious freak to believe in it/him. So, let me ask you this: You are postulating that there are infinite other universes out there, none of which I can measure, see, touch, taste, smell, hear, interact or verify. Why do you apply different standards for your belief than you apply to mine?

Are you sure you want to make this claim?

But worse for you (the atheist), with infinite universes that means every single possibility has occurred somewhere and there must be infinite identical copies of our Universe out there. Cosmologist Alexander Vilenkin says:

> A striking consequence of the new picture of the world is that there should be an infinity[30] of regions with histories absolutely identical to ours. Yes, dear reader, scores of your duplicates are now holding copies of this book. They live on planets exactly like our Earth, with all its mountains, cities, trees, and butterflies. The earths revolve around perfect copies of our Sun, and each sun belongs to a grand spiral galaxy – an exact replica of our Milky Way.[31]

This view may be possible, but is it reasonable? Aren't you being a superstitious irrational freak to believe that? And as an evangelist of your superstitious blind faith you want *me* to believe it, too? I don't think I have that much blind faith, especially when the alternative idea (God) seems to actually have other more verifiable evidence. In other words, when I start adding other proofs to Agent X being God, such as the Moral Argument, the Resurrection of Jesus, the accuracy of the New Testament, and so on, the weight of the evidence really lies with the theist. A person practically has to force himself or herself to believe in atheism and infinite universes. I'll expand on this in the Objections Appendix, where we discuss the almost ridiculous consequences of having to believe in an Infiniverse.

---

[30] His words, not mine, just in case someone was going to complain about my using the word "infinite."

[31] Alexander Vilenkin, *Many Worlds in One*, (New York: Hill and Wand, 2006), p. 112. As noted to me by RC Metcalf, from his book R.C. Metcalf, *Colliding with Christ: The Science of the Resurrection,* (Maitland, FL: Xulon Press, 2008). Available on Amazon.

Note that I am willing to accept multiple universes, but if you are an atheist you are forced to accept infinite universes and infinite copies of you and me.

But maybe the Singularity *is* Agent X!

Well the Singularity *itself* could **not** be Agent X, the cause of the Universe. Why? Because the Singularity is itself a mechanistic process. Any singularity that gives rise to a Big Bang will have done it in eternity past; any singularity that did not give rise to a Big Bang in eternity past will never do it in the future either. Thus to imagine that the Singularity is a non-mechanistic agent would require us to imagine that the Singularity has a volition and free will. In that case, the Singularity is much more than a singularity isn't it? It's a Being with a mind.

I should forewarn you that many people *still* continue to try to postulate mechanistic origins of the Universe. For instance, see Quentin Smith's attempted rebuttal in the Objections Appendix. Smith merely proposes another mechanistic agent as a cause of the first cause. That doesn't solve the problem. So, watch out for these attempts. They just push the problem back further. In short, you cannot eliminate the need for a non-mechanistic agent by postulating an *earlier* mechanistic agent.

Please note that as we go through this, I'm not saying the first cause was *caused*. It is the caus**er**. It's the uncaused caus**er**. Sometimes we use the words "the uncaused cause." What we really mean is "the uncaused caus**er**." This caus**er** had no *cause* of its own and was not caused. This notion matches up with the premises accepted by atheists 80 years ago mentioned previously, i.e., that everything that has a beginning has a cause; anything that existed forever needs no cause. Regardless of whether we view this from the theistic side or the atheistic side, we *both* are logically stuck with the fact that Agent X which caused the Universe, whatever it is, must have existed forever, *needs* no cause and *has* no cause.

What if nothing created the Universe?

If nothing created the Universe, you still have a problem. Why? Because "nothing" has no mind and is also mechanistic. And if "nothing" were going to create a universe, either it would have created it eternally ago, or it would have created infinite universes. Nothing helps nothing (pun intended).

What about an eternally old universe that is constantly collapsing and expanding?

This theory was actually and understandably proposed almost immediately by atheists after the discovery of the Big Bang. This idea tries to avoid the requirement for an eternal first cause. Unfortunately for the theory, all the recent research has shown that if the Universe were collapsing and expanding, we'd see residual energy after each event – but we do *not* see that. So this theory is currently scientifically *refuted*.

I will address Loop Quantum Cosmology in the Objections Appendix, but it's basically just another version of infinite universes. Remember LQC and infinite universes ideas require some pretty fantastical concepts, such as, every possible scenario has taken place, and there is a universe out there where you the reader actually wrote this book. Kudos are due you.

What if there's another option?

There can't be another option. As long as the Universe had a beginning (whether by the Big Bang or something else), we can clearly and logically conclude that the Universe was either caused by a mechanistic agent or it wasn't, there's no in-between. A partially mechanistic agent can't exist, because that would make it a *non*-mechanistic agent. This conclusion follows from the law of non-contradiction. It's irrational to disagree with it. If you start positing irrational things, you're being superstitious, not me, my friend.

And while we are talking about irrational things, remember nothing can create *itself*. Why? Because it would have to precede itself to cause itself. That's simply irrational. Do you really want me to abandon my argument for an irrational proposition? Besides, it would still be mechanistic. So it wouldn't help you anyway.

But if there was no time at the Singularity, how can we talk about eternity past?

We deal with this point in the Objections Appendix.

So let's add the newest characteristic that we've found out about Agent X to our list:
1. Agent X is eternal and exists forever.
2. Agent X needs no cause.
3. *Agent X is a non-mechanistic agent.*

Remember, our goal is to see if at some point we can triangulate and identify Agent X.

The Four Points
(1) The Universe had a beginning.
(2) The Universe is fine-tuned.
(3) The Universe has more than four dimensions.
(4) The Earth seems to have been placed in a precise location designed for easy scientific discovery of the Big Bang and Cosmology.

Chapter 4:
Fine Tuning

T he next item of relevance is scientists' discovering the Big Bang had to be so very finely tuned or it would have been a big flop. Think about it this way: creating the Universe turns out to be a very precise recipe – any change in any of its ingredients, or any change in the precise quantity of any ingredient and the whole thing falls apart.

Imagine using a recipe that required a precise ratio of 37 key ingredients. If you used minutely more or less of any of these 37 ingredients the recipe would fail colossally. Take the first ingredient, say sugar. This recipe calls for 28,600,000,000,000, 000,000,000, 000,000,000 lbs. of sugar.[32] That's 2.86×10^{31} lbs. If we say a sugar grain is the size of a grain of sand, then that would be roughly equal to all the grains of sand on 100,000,000 (100 million) Earths.

Now imagine that our recipe was so sensitive that if you added just one more grain of sugar than the exact amount to our mix, the whole monstrous cake would fall flat, or explode, or kill anyone who even tasted it. That's the degree of fine-tuning we have discovered in just the first ingredient, the ratio of electrons to protons. Other ratios in the Universe recipe are even more finely-tuned, if you can imagine that.

Thirty-seven known variables

Here's a list of 4 of the about 37 known variables (some scientists estimate there are over 200 such variables) and if they had

---

[32] Assume about a million grains of sugar in one pound so we have a ratio of $1:10^{37}$ grains

deviated from their currently known values by as little as what is shown in the table below, we'd not get a universe or we'd get a universe that has no heavy metals, or has no mass or expands too rapidly, or never expands and stays in a plasma form, or otherwise just doesn't work. The first ratio in the table is as exacting as the 100 **million** Earths example described above. The next ratio down is 1,000 times more exacting; it's like adding one additional grain of sugar in 100 **billion** Earths. The farther down you go, the more critical and finicky are the ratios. Now someone may complain, "Well, life may well have developed differently if these variables had been different." But do note carefully, we are not *only* talking about things localized to our solar system that affect life, like the Earth being too close or too far from the sun. In many we are talking about things that affect the *entire* Universe – like no Universe forming. So those are *not* anthropomorphically biased variables.

Ratio of Electrons to Protons $1:10^{37}$
> *if larger or smaller: chemical bonding would be insufficient for life chemistry.*

Ratio of Electromagnetic Force to Gravity $1:10^{40}$
> *if larger: stars would be at least 40% more massive than the sun; so stellar burning would be too brief and too uneven for life support;*
> *if smaller: all stars would be at least 20% less massive than the sun, and thus incapable of producing heavy elements.*

Expansion Rate of Universe $1:10^{55}$
> *if larger: no galaxies would have formed;*
> *if smaller: Universe would have collapsed prior to star formation.*

Mass of Universe $1:10^{59}$
> *if larger: overabundance of deuterium from Big Bang would cause stars to burn rapidly, too rapidly for life to form;*
> *if smaller: insufficient helium from Big Bang would result in a shortage of heavy elements.*

See the Appendix for the remaining 33
What do agnostic and atheistic astrophysicists say about all this?

Stephen Hawking:
> *The initial state of the Universe must have been very carefully chosen indeed. It would be very difficult to explain why the*

Universe should have begun in just this way, except as the act of a God who intended to create beings like us. [33]

Paul Davies:

There is for me powerful evidence that there is something going on behind it all...It seems as though somebody has fine-tuned nature's numbers to make the Universe ... the impression of design is overwhelming. [34]

Fred Hoyle:

A common sense interpretation of the facts suggests that a super-intellect has monkeyed with physics, as well as with chemistry and biology, and that there are no blind forces worth speaking about in nature. The numbers one calculates from the facts seem to me so overwhelming as to put this conclusion almost beyond question. [35]

Roger Penrose (mathematician):

I would say the Universe has a purpose. It's not there just somehow by chance. [36]

Note also: while two of the items listed above are required to support *human* life, the other two and many of the examples in the Appendix are parameters required for planets and galaxies to come into being and thus are requirements for *any* type of life to exist. Thus one can't escape these requirements by saying, "Well, life could have evolved in a different way."

So it seems that we can add one more characteristic to Agent X. It seems to know "enough" to fine-tune a huge functional universe. [37]

At this point some of you are thinking: "well, if we had infinite universes, each one with a slight variation on one of the

---

[33] Stephen Hawking, *A Brief History of Time: From the Big Bang to Black Holes*, (New York: Bantam Books, 1988), 127.

[34] Paul Davies, *The Cosmic Blueprint*, (New York: Simon & Schuster, 1988), 203. Davies may have since become a deist or a theist.

[35] Fred Hoyle, "The Universe: Past and Present Reflections," *Annual Review of Astronomy and Astrophysics*, 20 (1982): 1-35, 16.

[36] Penrose, R. 1992. *A Brief History of Time* (movie). Burbank, CA, Paramount Pictures, Inc.

[37] Note that while I rely upon astrophysicists to provide facts about the Singularity and the beginning of the Universe, it would be an "appeal to authority" fallacy to try to use an astrophysicist's opinions about God to try to prove that God exists. Just because someone like Einstein was a deist only reflects his opinion, it is not a logical or scientific proof. In this book, I am dealing with proofs and opinions within each authority's expertise.

ratios then eventually we'd get one where all the ratios work." While that is statistically true, we've already shown that the idea of infinite universes cannot be proven. Indeed, the idea becomes absurd when you realize that if there are infinite universes, that means there are infinite universes out there where you, if you are an atheist, are not an atheist but are in fact the author of *this* book and I'm the one disagreeing with it. Later in this book we develop points that further help put this notion to bed.

Okay, let's see what we know about Agent X so far:

1. Agent X is eternal and exists forever.
2. Agent X needs no cause.
3. Agent X is a non-mechanistic agent.
   To which we add:
4. *Agent X knows everything about the Universe and is able to create a fine-tuned universe.*

Neil Mammen

Chapter 5:
Multidimensionality and Extra-dimensionality

We can go a step further. In the instant 10^{-23} seconds after the Big Bang, we can calculate[38] that there used to be at least 10 dimensions. We know what four of the dimensions are. They form time and space (time, height, length and width). However, at the point of the Big Bang, that is "t_{BB}," calculations show the existence of up to 10 dimensions if not 26 (recently postulated in String Theory). At $t_{BB}+10^{-23}$ seconds, the tiniest instant after the Big Bang started, all but four of those dimensions disappeared. Note that the 26 dimensions did *not* exist within the Singularity. They only appeared *after* the Big Bang for that 10^{-23} second moment. They also don't exist *causally* prior to the Singularity. The word here is *cause*-ally not casually. They were not *caused* prior to the Singularity. So we say they do not exist outside the Universe.

Note that while time is a dimension, we are limited in time and can only go forward, so you could in a sense consider it ½ a dimension. However, the other 6 or 22 dimensions are all spatial dimensions (space-ial, i.e., in space). They are in some sense similar to our height, length, and width dimensions.

---

[38] Are you wondering how they figured this out? See Simon Singh, *Big Bang: The Origin of the Universe*, (New York: Fourth Estate, 2005). Also, the Large Hadron Collider in Switzerland has been designed to see if we can experimentally detect the presence of another dimension. Search the Internet to learn about the Kaluza–Klein theory.

But where are those other spatial dimensions?

Ah, that's a good question; we don't know where they are.[39] The best we can say is that they are "above" us, or rather, orthogonal to us.

Let me explain. Imagine if you were a two dimensional (2D) creature living on a piece of paper. In a 2D world there is only left and right, forwards and backwards. There is no up and there is no down. It's a flatland. Suppose that one day while walking you see a round brown object shimmering in front of you. You immediately try to capture it by building a wall around it. In 2D space, a wall is just a line because you can't go "above" it since there's no "up." A room in a flatland would be a square. So you build a square prison. You then put a locked door in the square knowing that nothing can go out or into the room except by the door. You then bring all the great scientists into the room and to your surprise, you see the brown circle start to change shape and get skinnier and finally it tapers off to a point and disappears.

"Impossible!" you exclaim.

"It's a ghost," shouts another.

When you tell the story, others think you were all hallucinating. "Well where did it go?" they ask. "Things don't just disappear."

"I don't know," you say, "I think it went to the *left*."

What had you seen? You had merely seen my 3D finger poking through the paper. And your measly walls and door were useless in imprisoning me. I just hopped over them.

In the same way, any 4D creature would be able to appear and disappear to us even inside a locked room. Just like I intersected the plane of your 2D world, a 4D creature could intersect the "space" of our 3D world, and appear and disappear at will.

A 3D cube and a 2D cube (a square)

Take a hollow cube; it exists in three spatial dimensions. But a 2D creature cannot comprehend what a cube is, because the creature has no concept of "up." If a 2D

---

[39] Scientists say one possibility is that they are curled up into tiny tiny balls. However, I focus here on what Dr. Kaku postulates in his book. Michio Kaku, *Hyperspace: A Scientific Odyssey Through Parallel Universes, Time Warps, and the Tenth Dimension*, (New York: Oxford University Press,

creature tried to explain where the *third* dimension was, it would say, "It's left" or something like that. But as far "left" as he went, he'd never find that other dimension.

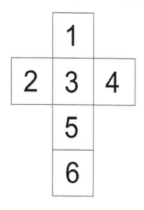

However, if I unfolded the cube into a flat piece of paper, a 2D creature would be able to comprehend the unfolded cube. It would see 6 flat squares as we see here.

When we folded up the squares in a certain way, we'd get back to the cube. The 2D creature would not understand how we could fold the cube up though.

A 4D cube and a 3D cube

Imagine that a 4 dimensional hollow cube existed, i.e., in 4 spatial dimensions; let's leave "time" aside for now. What would it look like? We have no real idea. But like the 2D creature was able to understand a 3D cube only when it was unfolded, perhaps we could unfold a 4D cube and comprehend what it looks like when it is unfolded.

A 4 dimensional cube is called a Hypercube or a Tesseract. So what would this 4D cube look like when unfolded? We can make some guesses. First, we note that a 2D cube is a square, has 4 sides, and each side is a line. A cube has 6 sides, each side is a square. So we'd expect a 4D cube to have 8 sides, and each side would be a cube.

Type	Dimensions	Sides	Type of Sides
Square	2 D	4	Lines
Cube	3 D	6	Squares
Hyper Cube	4 D	8	Cubes

So what does this hypercube look like when we unfold it? It should unfold into 8 cubes, shouldn't it? Now pause here for a bit. Try to imagine this *before* you turn the page.

Here you go:

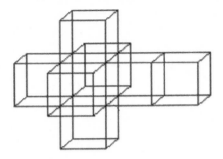

Notice it has 8 sides, and each side is a cube.
"But!" you object. "How does it fold back up?"
We actually don't know. We can't comprehend it.[40]

Is the Fourth dimension "up?"

In a way, yes, but you could go "up" as far as you want and you'd never find the Fourth Dimension. It's like the 2D creature saying "up" was "left." We are limited by our vocabulary.

Yet science tells us that at the point of the Singularity there were at least 6 other dimensions and maybe even 22 other dimensions.

This means that:

a. The concept of multi-dimensionality is not unscientific, i.e., many things *may easily* exist in 5 dimensions or more.

b. Notice that if a spatially 2D being which existed on a piece of paper were to try to hide behind a 2D object like a square, it would not stop you, a spatially 3D being, from seeing not only "behind" the square; you would see *inside* the square at all times. In fact, you could see inside the 2D being as well. Your presence in a sense would be everywhere the 2D creature could go. Thus, it follows that a being that had 4 dimensional senses would be able to see "over" anything that a 3D being would be able to hide behind. In other words, an n dimensional being can't hide from a $(n+1)$ dimensional being.[41]

---

[40] Actually, we could guess what it looks like as we rotate it into our plane. For more information, go to www.NoBlindFaith.com/AgentX/Dimensions.htm.

[41] Note in reality a 2D creature could hide from a 3D creature if it was far away. That's because the 3D creature shares the linear dimension and thus its limitations with the 2D creature. But an extra dimensional being would share no dimensions and thus have no

Interestingly enough, you could take a 3D basketball, and turn it inside out in 4D space without breaking it which would explain how you could get "inside" a 3D creature.

c. Thus, trying to caricature God/Agent X as an old man or trying to assign him a size is invalid. When she was 5 my daughter often asked me "How big is God?" "He's not physically big. He's outside the dimensions" I'd reply. It took her awhile to comprehend it, but it's true. Physical size is an invalid characteristic for Agent X. It's like asking how big an idea is. If you are talking about size then it's invalid. If you are talking about power and effectiveness, then you are on the right track.

d. Similarly this God is also not limited by smallness. In other words a microscopic creature is no smaller or inaccessible, invisible, or harder to see or interact for God than a whale or a large star like VY Canis Majoris. Size makes no difference.

e. All the dimensions that came into being are "inside" the Universe, i.e., they are part of the Universe. They did not exist before the Universe.

f. Thus, whatever caused or created the Universe and its multidimensional space is not within that space or time, nor is it constrained by it. In other words, Agent X, the cause of the Universe is *not* part of the Universe. It is not multidimensional but *extra*-dimensional. This by the way immediately eliminates any sort of pantheistic concept. In other words, science disproves pantheism (the idea that Agent X *is* the Universe and is mechanistic).[42]

g. The entity that created time is similarly "outside" of time. Therefore, Agent X is not constrained by time except by choice.[43]

For more information on multidimensional space and some great video clips and examples of how a hypercube may fold back up

---

limitations. This "seeing through and above" concept could also explain how "Every eye would see" when Christ returns. (*See* Rev. 1:7.) If His return is in 4D space and all our 4D senses are suddenly enabled, we could all see him, even if we are on opposite sides of the Universe. Just like if a 2D creature was able to see in 3D, nothing else in the 2D creature's world could block its view of the 3D event because we'd be "above" the 2D creature.

[42] I realize one could argue that Agent X could form part of Himself into a universe, but that is not pantheism but animism. Pantheism involves a concept of a mindless universe like George Lucas' amoral Force.

[43] Notably, William Lane Craig postulates that once God/Agent X created time he put himself into time and constrained himself by it, though being infinite and of infinite patience and of infinite knowledge it would not have any of the problems we might think it would have. Hugh Ross postulates the existence perhaps of an alternate time axis. I actually have not yet taken any particular position on this issue. I just need a bit more *time* to think about it. Sorry, that was too tempting.

into a 4 dimensional cube rotating into 3D space, go to:
www.NoBlindFaith.com/AgentX/Dimensions.htm.

A crucial point you must realize now: Agent X is **not** natural. Why? Because Agent X has to exist "before" time and space existed. That is, the first cause (the caus**er**) is not constrained by the 4 dimensions (what we call the natural) *or* the possible 26 dimensions (what we'd call supernatural). But we *can't* also technically say that Agent X is supernatural, because that would imply it is a superset of the natural, i.e., outside of the 4 dimensions but still constrained by the 26 dimensions. Yet we know that the first cause, Agent X, necessarily existed before any of the 26 possible dimensions because it pre-existed causally before the Big Bang.[44]

Is supernatural or extra-natural *unscientific?*

We can now say Agent X is "**extra**-natural." It's just **not natural** and it is not constrained by **any** of the dimensions in **any way**. Thus, the concepts of extra-natural and extra-dimensional are not only *scientific* but are also *necessary* characteristics of the first cause of the Universe.

Atheists can now **not** say that the supernatural, immaterial, non-mechanistic, or extra-natural is impossible, because science has just shown us that it is a *necessary* condition. Yet some atheists vainly cling to the old view:

> *Where science insists on material, mechanistic causes that can be understood by physics and chemistry, the literal believer in Genesis invokes unknowable supernatural forces.*
> ### Douglas Futuyma[45]

Futuyma's quote seems to completely ignore the multidimensional theories of the Big Bang.[46] Science doesn't insist everything is materialistic or mechanistic, it actually refutes that idea. The believer in Genesis is actually making appeals to facts that science has now in many ways said are possible.

---

[44] In case you think this is all merely romantic science fiction: the CERN Large Hadron Collider in Geneva, Switzerland, has been designed to see if we can interact with these other dimensions (amongst other things).

[45] Douglas Futuyma, *Science on Trial: The Case for Evolution*, (Sunderland, MA: Sinauer Associates, Inc, 1983), 12.

[46] One other reason why atheists cannot say the *un*-natural is impossible is abiogenesis. That term refers to the idea that life can come from non-life. The atheist has to admit that at some point in our history life came from non-life. More discussion of this detail appears in the Objections Appendix.

Here is another atheistic philosopher:

What I am asserting, however, is that anything that is real is, in the last analysis, explicable as a material entity or as a form or function or action of a material entity.

Philosopher William Halverson[47]

Material? Really? Are you sure you want to say that at the top of your voice? There's nothing natural or material (talking about 4D space and energy and matter) about the cause of the Universe or about the six other dimensions. And you can't beg off and say, "Well, 5D is still material." No it isn't. You can't taste it, smell it, feel it, see it, hear it, or measure it. Such other dimensions are exactly what we Christians have been calling the *supernatural* for the last 2,000 years and all the data seems to fit precisely. And this is what you atheists have been ardently claiming does *not* exist. Call it whatever you wish, but the cause of the Universe was not a normal event and the atheists must admit that even *they* have to rely on the existence of extra-natural, immaterial supernatural or unnatural events. So my question is: If one extra-natural immaterial event took place, in an eternity prior to the Universe, why not billions of extra-natural events? If you are going to abandon your principles for one event, why do you get to hold on to them for infinite and eternal events prior to that? Yet atheists do just that when they argue for infinite universes, and they must have blind faith to do so.

It proves at least one miracle is possible

The extra-natural Big Bang event eviscerates the claim that miracles are impossible. The common definition of a miracle is:

Miracle: an effect or extraordinary event in the physical world that surpasses all known human or natural powers and is ascribed to a supernatural cause.[48]

Suddenly the atheists appear caught in a bind. Any way you look at it, the Big Bang was an effect or extraordinary event in the physical world that surpassed all known human or natural powers and is ascribed to an unknown non-dimensional supernatural cause. That would qualify the Big Bang as a *miracle*. So we know that at least one miracle has happened. If one can occur, surely others can. What rationale insists that *only* one single solitary miracle could ever

---

[47] William H. Halverson, *A Concise Introduction to Philosophy*, Third ed. (New York: Random House, 1976), 394.
[48] http://dictionary.reference.com/browse/miracle

occur in all infinity (unless it occurred infinitely ago)? If one occurs, others can. Remember, any answer atheists provide must pass the mechanistic requirement or it fails their test.

What's worse for them is: anything that occurs as a result of any scientific interaction with the fifth supernatural dimension also qualifies as being a *miracle*. That means that other *miracles* can also happen. I don't think we can say that allowing for the supernatural is non-scientific anymore.

It refutes aliens

This line of reasoning also eliminates the idea that aliens created the Universe (not the panspermia concept as that's just localized to the creation of life). If they did, these aliens would have to be outside of time and space. And if someone really wants to promote this extra-dimensional aliens theory, all they are doing is creating a new religion with a set of gods that have powers similar to those of the Biblical God.[49] Their only claim to fame is that in this new religion, these gods don't want us to worship them. But there is less evidence for this religion than we have for Christianity. Considering all the evidence in an unbiased way, the "alien creators" idea is not as rational or as reasonable as the standard theist idea.

Time and Space

Next, we must realize that since the first cause is outside of the Universe, this first cause must also be outside of the constraints of time and space and outside of the Universe. Why do we say this? Because the first cause existed causally before space and time existed. Prior to the Singularity, there was no time or space. The first cause existed even before the Singularity, since it gave rise to the Singularity. Therefore, the first cause is not only outside of time and space, but it is currently unconstrained by space. (As a previous footnote stated, various philosophers think Agent X remains unconstrained by space but may now have made Himself constrained by time).

Please note the obvious: we must then conclude that Agent X exists outside of all dimensions since it existed before dimensions came to exist. In other words, Agent X is immaterial and does not

---

[49] Set theory shows us that logically *only* a single supreme being can exist, which eliminates the idea of "gods." Here's a quick explanation. A Supreme Being (S) is a being that has no equal. Thus for S to exist it has to be a single element set as any other element in that set would be equal to it, and would contradict the definition.

consist of matter or energy[50] nor is it bound by the multi dimensions of space and any of the other dimensions that physicists postulate. Agent X can therefore easily move in and out of these dimensions at will.

IMPORTANT: *This conclusion is true even if there are only 4 dimensions. We don't need any more than the natural dimensions to know that Agent X must be both extra-dimensional and also not composed of matter. Why? Because the cause of the Universe exists "before" and "outside" of the Universe.*

What we know about Agent X so far:
1. Agent X is eternal and exists forever.
2. Agent X needs no cause.
3. Agent X is a non-mechanistic agent.
4. Agent X knows everything about the Universe and is able to create a fine-tuned Universe.
5. *Agent X is not inside the Universe and is not constrained by space. Nothing inside the Universe can "hide" from Agent X.*
6. *Agent X is not composed of physical or universal matter.*

Other Interesting Points
As we end this chapter there are a few interesting side points to note. While not necessary to the argument, they should give us pause and are worth thinking about.

a. Multidimensionality is important because it explains how there can be a "spiritual" dimension. This could be a dimension that is outside of our 4D space. This dimension is a valid and logical physics concept. Whether it is populated by spirits or pink elephants is pure conjecture at this point, but we aren't trying to prove that, are we?

b. Hell and Heaven are not unscientific irrational concepts. Science has an easy way to explain how they *could* exist. They could be in other dimensions.[51] If there are up to 26 dimensions, then asking where Hell and Heaven are in 3D space only shows one's limited perspective. Heaven is only "up" in the way we might say the Fourth Spatial Dimension is "up" for us. It's more accurate to say it's

---

[50] Sure it could consist of some "other" type of matter and energy but this would not be anything that we'd recognize.

[51] Or in other universes if they exist as there. After this particular Universe is destroyed and a new one made from it, Heaven and Hell will still exist. This is why I say that there is good reason to think perhaps at least 2 other universes exist.

orthogonal. Similarly, Hell is only "down" in the same way. Can I prove this? No, but we can show Heaven and Hell existing in other dimensions is not unreasonable and fits the evidence. Should you use this as the only point to believe what the Bible says? Not at all. However, it does seem to indicate that this ancient text was cognizant of alternate dimensions before modern science came around to the concept. Not to beat this point into the ground, but: a being, limited to sensory perception in 3D space, would invariably describe something in another dimension as "up" or "out" there, just as a 2D being may be tempted to use the word "left" or "forward."

c. Beings like us humans could exist in 5 dimensions and if the beings had sensors and processors, they may only have these sensors in 4 of those dimensions and thus be unable to sense the 5th dimension. Imagine a still image camera on a tripod. *It* exists in time and 3D space, but it can only take 2D pictures and is limited in the "time" direction. The camera doesn't "realize" 3D exists. Note that a movie camera could take 2D + quantized[52] time pictures. In addition, if you move the camera in the third dimension and stitched those pictures together, you'd get quantized 3D (but the 2D camera would never be able to "comprehend" them because it could only register 2D pictures). Thus, while not provable, it is certainly within the realm of scientific possibility that human beings could be multidimensional, but not be able to sense all the dimensions in which they exist. Yes, exactly, just like a *soul*. In that case, asking why you can't measure or weigh or see the soul in 4D is like a 2D creature asking why they can't measure "up" in the x-axis or a still camera asking why it can't see time or measure it with a ruler. It doesn't have the capabilities.

d. Multi-dimensionality could allow the existence of life forms in these other dimensions. Such life forms might or might not intersect our dimensions. Multidimensionality could easily explain how Jesus could show up in a room with locked doors. He merely "hops" over in a fourth spatial dimension and back into ours. Just like a 3D creature would hop up into the third dimension to move past a 2D prison (a square drawn on the paper). This could also explain the "Spirit World" and indicate where Heaven is. It's not up, but orthogonal in a multidimensional space. The concept is fully rational. So where is Hell? Perhaps in another blend of dimensions that don't intersect ours. Can multidimensional beings intersect our

---

[52] Quantized means cut up into slices of time since the video camera only takes 30 frames per second (Okay, it's 29.97 fps to be exact. Having designed some of the first MPEG Video systems deployed back in 1992, you'd think I'd be precise).

space like angels and demons? Sure, it's scientifically plausible although currently not provable. When these beings did intersect our dimension, we would see them slowly or quickly appear, and when they leave our dimension they would shrink and disappear. This is similar to a 3D sphere intersecting a 2D paper. It will start as a point, grow to a circle, and then shrink back into a point. Similarly if you took a cube and passed it or rotated it through a plane, we'd see some very interesting shapes as the cube intersected the plane (unless you did it on one of the square ends, then you'd just see a square suddenly appear and then later suddenly disappear). Imagine now a 4D sphere intersecting a 3D space. We'd first see a dot, then we'd see a small sphere floating in midair, it would grow larger and larger until it reached the size of its 3D "diameter" then it would start to shrink down again and then disappear. A 4D creature could "fly" in this way, as they'd look like they were floating in thin air.

e. Given all this, death becomes merely a leaving behind of a limited 4D plane to a vastly better multidimensional plane. All we'd leave behind would be our "vessel."

f. You, as a 3D creature, could also be just as close as or closer to any 2D creature than any 2D creature could be to *another* 2D creature. How? Just by placing your hand on top of the 2D creatures. They would not sense it, see it, or know about it, and yet you'd be far closer to both of them in more places than they are to each other. In the same way, you could even be inside a 2D creature and influence it, as long as you were able to achieve that without destroying the 2D creature. Perhaps that is what is meant by being possessed.

g. This also means that there are at least two types of "spirits." Those that are multidimensional i.e. spirits that are *in* the Universe and a spirit that is *extra-dimensional* i.e. like the Holy Spirit - which precedes the Universe and matter. This latter one would be a spirit that is unconstrained by energy, matter or time or any of the dimensions.

As I said, these last few points are not part of the argument (and refuting them would not void the main point of this chapter, i.e., that there are dimensions and Agent X is outside the dimensions because he precedes them causally). Still, an important question we should ask ourselves is: How did the Bible and religious folks get it right? Why do these descriptions fit precisely something that took modern science centuries to realize?

Chapter 6:
Designed for Discovery

Earth seems to be in a very special location that facilitates "Scientific Discovery." This is our fourth point so let's look at the evidence.

a. Transparent Atmosphere

Many planets either have **no** atmosphere or have an opaque atmosphere. There's no requirement for life to **have** a transparent atmosphere. But there **is** a requirement for life to have a radiation protective atmosphere. We on Earth have one that is both transparent and protective. This allows us to actually see deep into space and study cosmology. Imagine if we lived under a heavy thick cloud cover and we never saw stars or the sun. Would the science of astronomy ever have developed? Remember that astronomy only developed as a science because amateurs took an interest and slowly developed tools and equations over time.

Astronomer Hans Blumenberg[53] said:

The combined circumstance that we live on earth and are able to see stars – that the conditions necessary for life do not exclude those necessary for vision, and vice versa – is a remarkably improbable one. This is because the medium in which we live is, on the one hand, just thick enough to enable us

---

[53] Hans Blumenberg, Robert M. Wallace (transl), *The Genesis of the Copernican Revolution*, (M.I.T. Press: Cambridge, MA, 1975) (1987 ed.).

to breathe and to prevent us from being burned up by cosmic rays while, on the other hand, it is not so opaque as to absorb entirely the light of the stars and block any view of the Universe. What a fragile balance between the indispensable and the sublime.

b. Our location in the spiral arm of the Milky Way Galaxy.

Too low, too deep or too close to the interior arms and we'd never be able to see past our own galaxy to discover the Big Bang. Why? Because all the other stars would ruin our view.

Astrophysicist Dr. Hugh Ross gives a great example. Imagine one of the closer nebulas known as SH2-215 was suddenly replaced by the Tarantula Nebula. We'd find out that at midnight we'd see shadows on the ground and Tarantula would cover the sky hiding all the galaxies behind it. No one would have discovered the Doppler shift in stars. Again, how far would astronomy and physics have developed? Would we have discovered the Big Bang? Not likely.

Remember there are far more solar systems deep inside galaxies with barely penetrable curtains of stars around them than there are planets on the fringes that allow for the greatest scientific discovery. Why aren't we on one of those?

c. We have a perfect tool to test relativity.

Albert Einstein,[54] the unknown patent clerk who became famous partly because of his theories of relativity, also proposed a way to prove that he was right. He said that his theory required light to be bent by gravity. Simply bring a very heavy object next to a light beam and you should see the light bend.

That is easier said than done. Where do we find a sufficiently heavy object? Well, we have the massive sun. If we could determine that the sun was causing light to curve, we'd know if this patent clerk knew what he was talking about. Here's the plan. First, we find a star that is behind the sun. Then we observe whether the gravitational pull from the sun causes the light from the star to curve around the sun. The theory says it should curve such that the star looks like it's to the side of the sun, not behind it. But there's a problem here. The sun is also a giant bright light source and if you try to spot a distant star right next to it you'd never see it.

---

[54] For a fun time go read his papers from 1905 here:
fourmilab.ch/etexts/einstein/E_mc2/www/ and fourmilab.ch/etexts/einstein/specrel/www

Unless we could blackout the sun.

But, if we blackout the sun with an object that is too big, it would cover the star's light. Remember the star is behind the sun to begin with and the curved light would show up only slightly to the side of the sun. On the other hand, if we try to blackout the sun with an object that is too small, then we won't cover the sun sufficiently and the light from the sun would overpower the light from the distant star. This experiment could work only if the object that we use to block the sun's rays with is exactly the right size and covers the sun perfectly. Not too small and not too large. That means the blocking object would have to be the same ratio in size to the sun as it is in the ratio of the distance to us from the sun.

Guess what? We have something. Yes, and you are already 3 seconds ahead of me. It's the moon. The moon just "coincidently" happens to be 400 times smaller than the sun and 400 times closer than the sun. This means we can get perfect eclipses of the sun. These eclipses allow us to verify various key facts about the gravitational effect on light and the composition of the sun. These facts allowed us to figure out color relationships and thus the red shift of the stars, and more. Solar eclipses allowed the world to realize that the strange ideas of this obscure patent clerk in Switzerland were correct.[55]

We have not yet found any other planets even in other solar systems or galaxies with the same relationship between their moons and their sun or suns.

Jay Richards further describes the importance of a perfect eclipse:

> ...these observations helped disclose the nature of stars. Scientists since Isaac Newton (A.D. 1666) had known that sunlight splits into all the colors of the rainbow when passed through a prism. But only in the 19th century did astronomers observe solar eclipses with spectroscopes, which use prisms. The combination of the man-made spectroscope with the natural experiment provided by eclipses gave astronomers the tools they needed not only to discover how the Sun's spectrum is produced, but the nature of the Sun itself. This knowledge enabled astronomers to interpret the spectra of the distant

---

[55] Some people have argued we could still have made this discovery with a larger or a smaller moon. However, as soon as you try this experiment yourself, you will see it isn't possible.

stars. So, in a sense, perfect eclipses were a key that unlocked the field of astrophysics....

And finally, perfect eclipses give us unique access to ancient history. By consulting historical records of past solar eclipses, astronomers can calculate the change in Earth's rotation over the past several thousand years. This, in turn, allows us to put ancient calendars precisely on our modern calendar system.[56]

Note the moon has also been moving away from the Earth, so there is an added coincidence, life on Earth would have to have "evolved" in the right timeframe to be able to utilize this feature. Evolve a few billion years too late and the moon is now too far away from the Earth to cover the sun, evolve a few billion years early and you have a moon that is so close to the Earth that it covers the sun and any stars that would have had their lights curve around the sun.

d. The equations[57] that define the Universe reduce to elegant and humanly comprehendible equations. There is no natural "requirement" for this to be so.

For example:

$$l^* = l\frac{1 - \frac{v}{c}cos\phi}{\sqrt{1 - v^2/c^2}}$$

Okay, you know its derivation simply as:

$$e = mc^2$$

In addition, this "elegance" allows us to know that we are getting closer to the "right answer." Let me elaborate. Mathematicians and physicists know almost invariably the "correct" answer ends up being an elegant answer. They have learned from

---

[56] http://www.discovery.org/a/2143

[57] My favorites though were always Maxwell's equations that described electromagnetic fields (light is electromagnetic radiation). In college I was a nerd and used to wear a T-shirt that said:

God said:

$\nabla \cdot \mathbf{E} = \frac{\rho}{\varepsilon_0}$

$\nabla \cdot \mathbf{B} = 0$

$\nabla \times \mathbf{E} = -\frac{\partial \mathbf{B}}{\partial t}$

$\nabla \times \mathbf{B} = \mu_0\mathbf{J} + \mu_0\varepsilon_0\frac{\partial \mathbf{E}}{\partial t}$

And there was light.

Yes, I know it looks complex to some, but I used to be able to derive the lot of them in under 15 minutes. I should add I believe the creation of light actually happened in Gen 1:1, not later as my T-shirt indicated i.e., when God said "Let there be light." More accurately is should be "Let the light be revealed". I think at that point, light already existed and it was just that the sun was revealed on the Earth.

experience: when their formulas get too unwieldy, they are probably missing something. In his book, *Big Bang: The Origin of the Universe*, Simon Singh discusses how they first started to suspect there were more than four dimensions. It was because the equations started to become more elegant as they added more dimensions into the mix.

e. Sufficient but not too many planets in the Solar System to allow us to track measure and calculate planetary mechanics as well as gravitational relationships.

Some solar systems only have 1 or 2 planets. Imagine if we had just a few or if we had too many, the early amateurs would have gotten completely confused when they tried to figure out all the effects of each planet on all the other planets. Yet we have just about enough to be able to figure out the cosmological relationships locally and then apply them universally. Remember, most original calculations were first done on paper without calculators.

The book by Jay Richards and Guillermo Gonzalez, *The Privileged Planet: How Our Place in the Cosmos is Designed for Discovery*, explores this in much more detail.

So, what does that tell us about Agent X?
It seems Agent X wants us to discover Him using Science – He wants us to develop science to find Him. He wants us to discover the red shift, the equations for relativity, and the Big Bang.

This is not fine-tuning!
Please note that this point should not be confused with the fine-tuning point previously discussed in an earlier chapter. Here's why: The fine-tuning points could be used to (weakly) argue that fine tuning is the only reason we are here to observe it. In other words, if the Universe weren't fine-tuned, then we wouldn't be here at all to see it. That viewpoint forces the infinite universe as the *only* solution for the atheist. After all, what are the chances that only one universe was ever attempted, and magically the first and only one worked?

The argument in this chapter is different, because there is absolutely no requirement for a universe that is fine-tuned to allow life to exist to also be fine-tuned to allow life to *discover* the origins of the Universe. If there is no intelligent agent behind it all, then the fine tuning and the ability to discover the origins are unrelated.

Notably, I am not saying Earth's location in the Universe is the *only* possible location for discovery. To suggest an intelligent agent planned it, our location needs only be a *sufficient* location.

It also need not be a perfect location; it just needs to allow us to make the discoveries. I do that with my daughter. I don't spoon feed her everything she needs to solve a problem. I want her to work to find the answers so that she will develop her skills and mature. In fact, she appreciates and dwells on the results more when she has to solve problems herself.

Massively fewer of these good locations for discovery exist than do bad locations. It's just yet another of those "fortunate" events. Remember also, many locations located out and away from other bodies would give us good places to discover science, but they are not protected from radiation and no conceivable life could survive there. We had to fit a slim set of necessary circumstances. See Hugh Ross's book, *Why the Universe is the Way it is* for much more information.

I also find this point eliminates from reasonability the infinite universes idea. Is it reasonable to think that, of all the universes out there, we just managed to end up on that is perfect for scientific study? Why didn't we end up on one of the other universes where the Earth is not in such a convenient place in the Universe? It's just a bit too fishy. Yes, it is *possible*, just like it is possible that we all suddenly popped into being 30 seconds ago with our memories artificially programmed into us. But is it *reasonable* to think that? I don't think so. Why do *you* think so? We cover more about this in the Objections Appendix showing that it's actually superstitious to believe in infinite other universes that you can't see taste, hear, touch, measure, sense, or calculate.

What we know about Agent X so far:
1. Agent X is eternal and exists forever.
2. Agent X needs no cause.
3. Agent X is a non-mechanistic agent.
4. Agent X knows everything about the Universe and is able to create a fine-tuned universe.
5. Agent X is not inside the Universe and is not constrained by space. Nothing inside the Universe can "hide" from Agent X.
6. Agent X is not composed of physical or universal matter.

7.   *Agent X for some reason wishes us to discover the Big Bang and thus confirm His existence and did so by designing a planet for mankind in time and space that would allow man to discover Agent X.*

Chapter 7: Conclusion

We shall call (and have been calling) this first cause "Agent X." Note that we are free to call it anything we wish as long as we establish that it is a free will agent capable of creating a Universe (including the time dimension). In addition, we must conclude that this free agent is outside the Universe and has dominion or full control and power over the Universe.[58]

The Four Points Revisited

As we said, we would cover these four major points:

a. The Universe had a beginning
b. The Universe is fine-tuned.
c. The Universe has more than 4 dimensions.
d. The Earth seems to have been placed in a precise location designed for easy scientific discovery of the Big Bang and Cosmology.

Given these four points, we've reasoned that Agent X has the following characteristics that we have derived:

1. It exists without cause:

This means it is Eternal and Uncaused.

2. It is a free will non-mechanistic agent:

This means it has to have a mind.

3. It is not constrained by time or space:

This means it is Omnipresent in space and all dimensions, i.e., it is Omnipresent *in* the Universe.

4. It is powerful enough to create a universe:

This means it is Omnipotent *for* the Universe.

5. It is knowledgeable enough to create a finely-tuned universe where even minute changes in values of things like the gravitational field would result in an unlivable or non-existent universe:

This means it is Omniscient *about* the Universe.

---

[58] It is hard to believe that this free agent created the Universe by accident and has no control over it - but I guess that is an option - just not one that I have spent much time on.

6. It is not composed of physical or universal matter as it causally preceded all universal matter in *all universes:* **This means it is a non-material Spirit Being.**
7. It wants us to discover it:
This means it is Personal.

None of these are theological conclusions; they are rational logical and scientific conclusions. The evidence led us here.

Now I don't know about you, but if something is an Eternal, Uncaused, Omnipresent, Omnipotent, Omniscient and a Personal Spirit Being with a Mind, that definition does not fit the definition of a lepton or hyperspace or yet to be discovered particle. Any being or thing with these characteristics is what I'd define as *God.* Call it what you may, but only God has those characteristics.

Thus, we should not see this as a statement of faith, but just one of derivation. It's a logical derivation of the necessary characteristics of the first cause.

This derivation is equally valid – I would say more rational – than the atheists' derivation that the Universe is rebounding cyclically or is formed by buds or that there are infinite universes. None of these can be proven at this time (actually, the cyclical rebounding universe is disadvantaged because current evidence indicates it **cannot** happen). And it's simply unreasonable for me to imagine there are billions of copies of me and you out there. But if you accept the atheists' views, then that's your *only* other option.

An atheist has to have more faith

The table is turned. Based upon all we've discussed here, the statement, "I believe there is *no* free will non-mechanistic extra-dimensional Agent" (the atheistic view) is a statement of blind faith.

Why?

Because it believes, **contrary** to scientific evidence, that the Universe is a result of infinite previous collapsing and rebounding Universes or that, the Universe has no cause, when we know that it requires a non-mechanistic cause. We can only calculate one universe and can only prove one universe scientifically. In other words, you have to have faith to believe something contrary to all the evidence we have. Nothing in the evidence can show there is *no* first cause; all the evidence points to a first cause.

Neil Mammen

I guess you can harbor a strong hope and blind faith that future evidence will someday come to light that disputes the current Big Bang cosmology.

This Agent X is not necessarily the God of the Bible

Please note that at no time have I made a direct case for the God of the *Bible,* nor have I provided any arguments that prove that Jesus is God. I have made a case only for an eternal God, a supreme free will non-mechanistic agent that is not constrained by time or space, which can create a universe. We've called it Agent X. The case for the God of the Bible and for Jesus is saved for other books in this series. However, we *have* shown that the Judeo-Christian Bible has had a more accurate view of the Universe than science itself had for thousands of years. The Bible's view differed greatly from the views of every other religion except Islam (which borrowed its view from Christianity). This fact should cause honest atheists some concern.

But where did Agent X come from?

Now the big question that everyone asks is: But where did God *come* from? What was before God? Kids ask that, atheists ask that. We ask that.

The short answer for this is: That's a stupid question.

Okay, we really do need to answer it. From reasoning we answer: Agent X did not come from anywhere because it did not **need** to come from anywhere. Remember one of the derived conclusions about Agent X is that it is not constrained by time or space.

Here is the full explanation

We have called the cause (the caus**er**) of the Universe *Agent X.*

The Universe consists of both time and space. Thus, Agent X is the cause of time. 13.7 Billion years ago, causally, before the Singularity, there was no time. This is a scientific theory that most atheists must accept if they give any heed to science. (If they don't, then we are back to faith – aren't we?)

So let's think this through: Agent X is the cause of everything. Therefore, Agent X caused time to exist. As discussed above, science shows us that when the Universe did not exist, time did not exist. So, if Agent X caused time (and space and the Big Bang), that means Agent X is not bound by time and instead causally existed before time. And similarly, Agent X is also not bound by space and thus existed without space.

The questions again: Where did Agent X come from? Why does Agent X not need a beginning? What was before Agent X? And the answer is:

There was no "before" before Agent X caused time, so the question has no meaning. There was no "from" before Agent X caused space, so again the question is meaningless.[59]

Let me say that again because I've had people say: Huh?

There was no "before" before Agent X caused time, so the question has no meaning.

There was also no "from" before Agent X caused space, so the question has even less meaning.

You see you need "time" to have a "before" and you need "space" to have a "from.""

But the instant "before"[60] Agent X caused time and space, the instant "before" the Singularity or even *in* the Singularity, the words "before" and "from" had no meaning. In fact, the word "instant" had no meaning because there was no time. In fact, the word "in" had no meaning either for that matter because there was no space either... Whoops, the word "had" had no meaning either.

However you look at it, "before" Agent X caused time, the words "before" and "from" had no meaning.

You see, if you are asking a spatial or temporal question we can't even describe or explain because we lack the ability to imagine it, and we lack the words to describe it, then we might as well forget about understanding it fully. However, you can see why I think this is a rational answer to the question. Don't feel like you have to accept it, but it **is** quite scientific.

Scientifically we would say: Causally before the Singularity, the word "temporally before" had no meaning. Therefore, it is meaningless to ask what was temporally before the Singularity. It is just as meaningless to ask where the first cause of the Singularity came from. But note that it is *not* meaningless to ask what "caused" the Singularity, because we know the Singularity as a mechanistic

---

[59] William Lane Craig says: "Notice that I am not saying that this Being existed before the Big Bang temporally. He is *causally* prior to the Big Bang, but not *temporally* prior to the Big Bang." http://www.leaderu.com/offices/billcraig/docs/jesseph-craig2.html

[60] Again, we are stuck with having to use words that are really meaningless in a timeless dimensionless singularity.

agent could not have existed in timeless eternity and then suddenly caused the Big Bang. (See all our reasons above about why non-mechanistic agents can't explain the cause.) So, while Agent X is causally prior to the Singularity, it is **not** temporally prior to the Singularity. Yes, it boggles the mind, doesn't it?

In addition, when people ask: Where did Agent X come from? The answer could also include this statement: Before Agent X created space, the words "where" and "from" had no meaning, so what is your question exactly?

So let's go return to what **atheists** used to say:
Anything that began to exist needs a cause. Anything that existed forever needs no cause.

Well, God did not begin to exist, He has always existed. Thus, God needs no cause and God was not made by anything. It fits the atheists' own formula. If something had always existed, there is no event causally or moment temporally that precedes its existence, thus it could not have a cause. It would seem illogical to argue against this definition.[61]

But you may object about the entire conclusion

You may try to argue: "We don't know if an alternative theory will arise that will be provable that shows that the Universe is infinitely old, or that there are infinite numbers of them. Science continues to evolve. Remember we used to think the world was flat."

Yet atheists' materialist arguments must rely upon the current state of science. So, if you are depending upon some "new" theory to be proven in the future, then you are depending on blind faith. I personally don't like any sort of blind faith. I'd like to go with the more rational and logical explanation. Actually, this waiting for a new theory can be a game. If you want to wait until science disproves itself, why can't we wait a bit longer until science disproves itself *again*? How long do we wait and how long do you blindly believe what is unscientific, hoping to be rescued from the God concept? That "new future theory" argument is a "science of the gaps" theory: If I don't like the current answer, then I'll just say that

---

[61] You could dispute the definition, but then we would be arguing that "nothing eternal exists," not that "nothing eternal has a cause." And this doesn't help the atheist, as he also needs something eternal to exist, such as a mechanistic agent or infinite universes. He could try to default to nothing created the Universe, but he would return again to a mechanistic agent. And how much *more* superstition is needed to believe *nothing* created *everything*?

we'll find the answer I like later and ignore the current rational conclusions.

Remember, you are not saying that you "don't know" the answer. You are saying that you *know* the current scientifically proven answer but dislike the consequence of that logic. Where will you draw your line on rejecting science? You're also taking a hypocritical stance; did you ignore the provability of various biological processes while you were "waiting for a better theory?" Why not wait for a better answer when it comes to evolution? Evolution constantly has to make amendments to its basic theories as we learn more and more about science, yet why not say: "Oh, we'll wait to see if an intelligent designer shows up." Perhaps the reality is that your biases, fears, and distastes are forcing you to blindly reject rationality and to be unscientific.

Frankly, people who have blind faith in things that are unscientific scare me (Okay, I just had to say that – but it is in fact very close to the truth – go to www.NoBlindFaith.com and look up *Mythbusters: Blind Faith* for why I think that).

Notice how this argument and its conclusion also leave the rational agnostic with no room to be *agnostic* about the *existence* of God. This book provides the evidence that you thought was not available. If you continue to claim to be an agnostic, you are doing so contrary to reason and science. You are a blind faith agnostic who hangs on to your agnosticism in the face of logic.

But how do we know that logic and rationality are transcendent and exist outside the Universe?

One skeptic asked me, "Once you get before the Singularity we don't know anything about anything. So how could we say that logic and rationality still apply? Maybe they came into being simultaneously?"

My answer, "Let me ask you this. In the instant before the Universe came into being at the Big Bang, did that Universe exist in the same form as it would be an instant later after the Big Bang?"

He looked at me quizzically, "No, of course not."

"Ah," I said, "Now would you say that's a logical conclusion? Would you say that that was logically true the instant before the Universe came into being? Before the Universe existed, could you write the equation: '*No Universe* is not the same as one Universe?' Or to put it simply: 'Zero is not equal to One?' That equation states the law of non-contradiction – did that law exist before the Singularity? And most importantly, are you trying to *rationally* argue that *irrationality* is transcendent?" That took a bit of processing for him. Finally I said, "Look I've given you a very systematic case. I've provided you with the facts and your best response is 'Irrationality is true.' Surely you are clutching at straws here. I thought the Christians were supposed to be the irrational ones."

Have the honesty to agree that you have a dilemma

In a debate between my friend, Christian apologist Frank Turek and the bombastic, wordy, rambling late atheist Christopher Hitchens, they were each asked, "What would it take for you to change your mind?"

Turek essentially said, "Well if we found out that the Big Bang was wrong *and* this Universe had indeed existed forever,[62] I'd start to have to re-evaluate things, because for one that would indicate the Bible was wrong."

Hitchens' response was "Nothing."

Get that? Nothing could change his mind!

Similarly, after I presented some of this information on multidimensional space to a relative who is an atheist, I expected something like, "Hmm, I guess there could be other dimensions. It is curious that the Bible knew this 4,000 years before science finally figured it out. I guess that insisting that only what I see, touch, hear, etc., is the only reality that exists, is not only unscientific but it's almost religious."

Instead, he said, "Well, I think you are going too far."

Going too far? *Going too far?* At least have the integrity to agree that you've been *wrong* all this time on this one issue and that you need to do some serious re-evaluation. Talk about unscientific irrational close mindedness. Talk about the stubborn audacity of blind faith.

Do you see why I think that most atheists are sadly unscientific and close-minded and become irrational when the evidence goes against them? I hope you will prove me wrong and admit that there are problems with what you've believed until now. Remember: Don't let the consequences of good logic force you to abandon that logic.

---

[62] Notice he's not talking about infinite collapsing and expanding universes here.

Summary

In conclusion, we started with "Who is Agent X," and asked what the characteristics of X were.

I postulated that Agent X was separate from God to begin with, but at the end of this, we conclude that Agent X has all the characteristics of a longstanding traditional description of God. Therefore, we have to conclude that it is most reasonable and rational to think that Agent X **is** God.

Given this, it seems that is also takes faith to be an atheist and in light of the other proofs about Christianity (see www.NoBlindFaith.com), it would seem that the atheists might also have the deck stacked against their beliefs (or lack thereof).

Chapter 8:
Afterthought – How can God Listen to *All* our Prayers at the Same Time?

One common complaint people make about the concept of God is: How can He listen to *all* our prayers at the same time. I saw an atheist mock this on his website. He said, "This God will go crazy if He can hear all our prayers, won't it be deafening for Him?" Bill Maher asks this question in his anti-Christian movie "Religulous" [sic]. Maher essentially says, "Oh, and we are supposed to believe that there's this old white bearded man up there listening to all 6 billions of our mutterings."

Bill Maher should do a bit more reading.
This is simply an irrational complaint once we understand extra-dimensionality.

If God is not constrained by time,[63] then He can listen to *all* 6 billion of our prayers at the same "time." In fact, He can attend to each one of us individually. C.S. Lewis explained it vividly back in the 1950s:[64]

Suppose I am writing a novel. I write "Mary laid down her work; next moment came a knock at the door!"

For Mary who has to live in the imaginary time of my story there is no interval between putting down the work and hearing the knock. But I, who am Mary's maker, do not live in that imaginary time at all.

Between writing the first half of that sentence and the second, I might sit down for three hours and think steadily about Mary. I could think about Mary as if she were the only character in the book and for as long as I pleased, and the hours I spent in doing so would not appear in Mary's time (the time inside the story) at all.

---

[63] Various philosophers that I respect, such as William Lane Craig, suggest that God invariably had to constrain Himself by time after he created us, in other words, He entered into time. But this still allows Him to halt time if He wishes, just like a programmer can freeze a program that he's debugging.
[64] C.S. Lewis, *Mere Christianity*, (San Francisco: HarperOne, 2001) (3d ed.)

In fact, some ancient Jewish Rabbis had this idea well established. They said, for instance, that the 10 Commandments were not given in order. They were given all at *once*, simultaneously in time. They did not think temporal sequentiality (time sequence) would be a limitation for an extra-dimensional being.

So Christians, when you pray, pray in earnest, for you have the Creator of the entire Universe's undivided attention, attending to you individually and personally. And when you sing praises next week in church, sing in earnest, as He is focusing on and listening to you *alone* and as the Westminster Confessional implies, He is enjoying you as you enjoy Him.

Maher[65] really needs to get out of his rut and do a bit more reading before he embarrasses himself at the top of his voice.

Hamlet and Shakespeare

Remember our discussion about Kant. Kant said that you *Kant* prove that God exists using science (pun intended). You see, that is true if and only if God *doesn't* want us to discover Him. C.S. Lewis made a very interesting comment about the relevance of God being "outside" the Universe. He said if God is outside of our dimensions then, looking for God *in* the Universe is like Hamlet[66] running around looking for Shakespeare. He's not going to find Shakespeare there unless Shakespeare has written *himself* into the play. This is why we *can* use science to discover Him.

May I suggest that God did *indeed* write Himself into this play? By leaving clues to the Big Bang, by designing our world for discovery, and by sending Jesus Christ?

---

[65] By the way, if you know Maher, tell him that I, an unknown engineer, would love to challenge him to a debate about Christianity in front of a mixed audience where we each get equal time. I suspect that once you take the reins away from Maher and put him where he can't control the situation, he'll either weasel out of it or bail because he knows that he'd lose miserably if engaged on equal ground. It's easy to win a stacked fight.

[66] The character Hamlet, not the actor playing him.

Chapter 9:
What's Next?

There are five steps in this journey.

In this book, we proved that it's more reasonable to think God exists. But, as we said, if God does exist, that does not mean He's the Christian God. He could be the Muslim god or one of the three million plus Hindu gods, or even the great spirit of the Native Americans.

We know however that He could not be the deist's[67] god because we've already determined that He wants us to discover Him.

So how do we determine whose God He is? Or to be more precise, which religion (if any) is *His* true revelation. Does it even matter which religion we follow? Are all religions essentially the same? Is all religion merely blind faith and independent of facts? These questions carry implied assumptions that many people believe without any rational thought.[68]

In another book in this series, *No Blind Faith*, we discuss how all other religions expect and require you to have blind faith to believe in them. We show how only Christianity insists that blind faith is not only bad, but is sinful. The Bible documents many occasions when God punished the Israelites for having blind faith.[69] That motivates us to decide there is indeed value in focusing on the one religion, Christianity, which claims it can prove itself factually, historically,

---

[67] A deist is one who believes that God exists but does not interact on a personal basis with us. While many claim Thomas Jefferson and Benjamin Franklin of our founding fathers were deists, they did not act like deists, from what we learn about their documented prayers to God asking Him to interact personally with the creation of the United States. Note too that most of the other 57 founding fathers were not only strong Christian believers but some were even ordained ministers. *See* John Eidsmoe, *Christianity and the Constitution: The Faith of Our Founding Fathers*, (Grand Rapids, MI: Baker Academic, 1987).

[68] Before you can actually start to witness to someone, you have to deal with these preconceptions or it'll short circuit anything you tell them about God or Jesus.

[69] Look at the passages where God describes all the physical things He's done for Israel, like parting the Red Sea, the pillar of fire, manna, and water in the desert. Yet they go out and worship idols that they made themselves idols, which can't do anything. Then God punishes the Israelites for blindly following those idols despite His proof.

and logically without a basis in blind faith. Do these claims have any validity? Consider the following steps in the thought process.

Step 1 is "Proving Blind Faith is a bad idea and Rational Faith[70] is the only good option."

This step includes proving that all religions are *not* the same in what they teach and that all other religions require blind faith. Christianity and its parent, Judaism, are the only religions that condemn blind faith.

Yet, once we've proved Blind Faith is bad, how do we prove that Christianity isn't a blind faith just like all the other religions? We do this with apologetics,[71] which is the defense of the faith (not an apology for it).

The first apologetic would be to prove that God exists. After all, if God does not exist then the entire discussion is of no value.

Note a very important point here: I think proving the existence of God is the primary thing to do first in any argument about Christianity.[72] Why? Because if I can prove to someone that there exists an intelligent first cause of the Universe, then everything else that Christians claim becomes plausible. The greatest miracle ever recorded was not the Resurrection, it was not Christ's birth, it was not Jonah and the whale, it was not the flood, it *was* the creation of the Universe.

Why is this? Because if God exists and can create the entire Universe, surely He can raise someone from the dead. Especially if it's just some multidimensional activity and reattachment of a 5 dimensional soul into a 4 dimensional shell (the body). This Entity could also easily use energy matter conversion to feed 5,000 people; He could easily heal someone using matter regeneration. After all, if you can envision, design, architect, and create matter out of nothing,

---

[70] Rational Faith is the concept that your faith should be akin to *trust*. You should never blindly trust anyone. Your faith should be based on facts, logic, reason, and experience. Faith and trust need to be earned. While emotions are important for relationship, they are dangerous for evaluating the trustworthiness of anything. Con men are most successful because they make their victims "feel" secure. Don't be conned into a religion. Test all things; hold on to that which is true (not to that which gives you a good gut feeling). 1 Thessalonians 5:21 (KJV) confirms this approach.

[71] From the Greek, "*apologia*," meaning to defend or explain, as written in 1 Peter 3:15.

[72] Note this is not *the* most important thing. Remember that just as important is that you gain their respect and allow them to understand that you care about them before you move forward. That's why one of the legs in our motto is "Relationship."

then surely you can regenerate and manipulate that same matter. He can also easily preserve someone alive for a few days in a large sea creature.

In one sense, if I can prove God exists, then arguing about evolution becomes less important. The creation-evolution discussion would mainly examine God's means for making and diversifying biological life.

So step 2 is "Proving that it is reasonable to think God exists" (this book).

But even if it is rational to think God exists, that doesn't mean that He's the God of the Christians. We need some way to isolate which religion's God He is, if any. Maybe He has not revealed Himself yet. So we will first investigate the claims of the Christians to see if they can prove that their God is the actual God. We start this by looking at what Christians claim is a document given by God, the Bible. Where did it come from? Is it even accurate?

So step 3 is "Proving that the Christian Bible we have today is indeed what the original author's wrote; using history, archeology, and forensic methods."

But now let's say we manage to prove the Bible is what the original authors wrote, yet that doesn't mean they weren't lying and wrote it for power or fame. It also doesn't preclude that it was some big misunderstanding or that Jesus wasn't a con man who fooled the apostles into thinking He rose from the dead.

So step 4 is "Proving that it is rational and reasonable to believe that Jesus physically rose from the dead using history, archeology, and medical science. This would prove that what the apostles wrote is true and that Jesus really was telling the truth and really is God."

Okay, if you prove all that, we still have some important questions like: Why did Christ have to die? Why must this God punish Sin? What about Evil and God?

Step 5 is "Teaching them the Theology"[73] (the details).

---

[73] Notice that Theology must be internally *and* externally consistent. Why do I say that? Because you can write a fiction novel that is internally consistent. For instance J.R.R. Tolkien's "Middle Earth" is pretty internally consistent, but that doesn't make it a real

a. Explaining why Christ had to die and why God must punish sin. Explaining why a good God would send people to Hell.
b. Explaining why God *must* be good, i.e., dealing with Euthyphro's Dilemma.
c. Explaining how there can be a good God that allows evil and suffering to exist. This also explains the death of children.
d. Responding to the seemingly paradoxical questions like: Can God create a stone so big that He cannot move it?

These are the 5 steps in evangelizing and witnessing to others. By using the Columbo Tactic referred to in the Appendix, they can all be done without ever feeling uncomfortable. Books on these topics will be available in the No Blind Faith series. In the meantime, you can download papers on them at www.NoBlindFaith.com.

---

world. True theology must have *externally* consistent facets. For instance, when we say "Man has a sin nature," the evidence for that sin nature is discoverable even in two-year old babies.

Appendix I:
Atheist Objections

Many people read this information and have lots of objections.

I chose not to cover all the objections in the main text, as it would then become long, wordy, and hard to follow. But the objections are very important. Over the years, many atheist friends and not so friendly ones (on the web or by email) have reviewed this content and tried to attack its premises. This section covers most of what people have asked in the past (see especially Objection 8).

If I've missed your objection here, please feel free to email it to me at **agentXobjections@NoBlindFaith.com** and I will do my best to address it genuinely. If you can prove to me that I am wrong, I do not wish to hang on to a myth. I have better things to do with my time, my money, and my passions.

Most of the entries here were written as emails in response to objections from individuals. Thus, the tone of the response will usually reflect the tone of the original objection (some objections were really snooty as you can imagine) or will be a response to a Christian who was given the objection by a friend of theirs. If you are an atheist, I ask that you forgive the tone of some of these responses and do not let it turn you off. I've worked on rewording some of these to be less "in your face." You will occasionally notice repeated responses, as some objectors would miss or misunderstand entire sections of the original write-up, forcing me to repeat myself. But I understand that, because I'm guilty of it too. I see something I disagree with and I just skim it. However, I urge all readers not to just skim this material, as it should answer most of your objections.

By the way, some may feel that a few of these questions are "straw men," i.e., artificial arguments I invented to easily knock down. But they really aren't. Many of these were directly copied emails that I've edited just a little for clarity and poise.

Objection 1. If God exists, then why is there so much evil in the world?

Response: Actually, this objection requires a book of its own. But think about it: if we can scientifically prove that God exists, then we can surely derive other valid reasons why evil exists (see our other upcoming books in this series). Just because you don't like Him or what He does, it surely doesn't mean He cannot exist. I recommend we first address the fact of whether God exists and then decide the theological implications of this God existing. It's akin to arguing about what kind of tail a pink flying unicorn has when we can't even agree if the unicorn exists. Let's decide if it exists first, then we can argue the details, if it makes sense to even argue further. However, if you want a preview, go to NoBlindFaith.com and look up "Evil and God." In that paper I show this Objection 1 is a "suicide statement," that is, asking the question refutes its very premise.

I do want to address one issue that seems to come up repeatedly. It is the whole issue of God's killing people or letting 50 children die in a natural catastrophe. That is, evil that is "done or commanded by God" versus evil done by men committed by their own free will. Many atheists keep positing this question as though it's a stumper. They keep pointing to passages in the Bible where God asked the Israelites to kill thousands of people, or described how God struck people dead. They urge that these passages show either that God does not exist or that we are inconsistent about God. Some atheist writers say God is "evil" for doing this (although that is a self-refuting "suicide" statement[74]).

Death is not the End Game!

I was once at lunch with a group of engineers when the topic of God came up, and someone mentioned that I was sort of a "preacher man." Immediately a very loud chap two seats over announced, "Are you religious? Well, I don't believe in God,

---

[74] The charge is self-refuting because you can't call something "evil" if there is no standard of good and evil. There can't be a standard unless it comes from someone who has the authority to create the standard. Since neither you nor society has the authority to create an absolute standard, you are left with the standard being just a preference – and there is no good reason why God or anyone else should adhere to your or my preferences. But the fact that you recognize that a standard exists indicates that *you think there is an objective moral standard*, which can only come from an authority above mankind such as the Creator. But that's precisely whose existence you are trying to disprove. Your statement refutes itself.

because, last week 50 children died in an earthquake in Italy. You tell me how you align that with your God!"

I looked at him, and said, "I'm sorry for the death of those children, but let me ask you this. If there *is* a God, where did all those children go when they died?"

He paused. Long silence. Everyone at the table stopped eating. I could sense the wheels churning. More awkward silence. People even stopped chewing.

He said after a while very timidly, "With God?"

I said, "Yes, and in fact they went to a far greater place than they'd ever been before. You see if God exists, death is not our final destiny; it's not that terrible thing that you think it is. We go to better place, far better than anything we can imagine."

Long pause. Then to my utter surprise, he said very quietly, "I understand."

Everybody went back to eating.

I'd never had that happen before. We became friends.

You see, once you realize that God is omnipresent and the creator *and* that there are other dimensions, then we realize that death is merely the leaving of one's old shell here on a limited plane and going to a far better space with more colors, more sounds, more flavors, more senses and more love. It's not the End Game![75]

In light of this, asking why God can't rightfully transport someone from one dimension to another borders on ludicrous. Remember that you don't *have* a soul. You *are* a soul; you *have* a body. A weak measly corruptible body that will be replaced one day when it falls apart. And consistent with your insistent demands, we actually do believe God never ever "kills" anyone multi-dimensionally or eternally. He never destroys your soul. You will exist as *you* for all eternity.[76] You will never die. God will never truly kill you. That can be a scary thought for some.

So, to be logical, if you are going to question a Christian's philosophy, you have to first consider if it is consistent with his other beliefs. This Objection is not a gotcha question; it's a cliché that doesn't survive scrutiny. You may not accept our beliefs, but you

---

[75] Even 5 year olds understand this when Great Grandma goes away on a journey to be with God. And, no, I can't prove this, but it does follow logically from Christian theology. It is self-consistent.

[76] Yes, I have to admit there are some annihilationists amongst Christians but I think that is more of an aberrant belief system and cannot be supported by Scripture.

surely should examine them and understand how they relate. You'd be hard pressed to refute this logic within its frame of reference.

Now *you* as an individual can't morally transport someone (without justification) from one dimension to another (kill him) because that would be akin to kidnapping, i.e., moving him without his permission. Yet, the Creator could do it anytime and anyplace without it being wrong. What is more important, the Creator could legally, logically, and rationally authorize His agents to act for Him to move people out of the natural dimensions. That is the case with the death penalty and what God commanded the Israelites to do in the Old Testament. Now of course, the problem in the latter case is that one must be able to validate 100% that those agents *really* heard from the Creator and it isn't blind faith and they aren't being brainwashed by some twisted charismatic leader (like the 9-11 hijackers). However, just because you and I require evidence from the human to prove he is in communication with the Creator, that does not and cannot invalidate the logical justification of the Creator, if He exists, to rightfully take those actions if He saw fit. Can we agree on that?[77]

My atheist friends, may I good-naturedly tell you that you really need to stop thinking *inside* the box with your limitations. Certainly *you* think that death is this awful horrible thing. But in reality that's like a child thinking that when Daddy leaves for work in the morning, she'll never see him again. But when she's 3, she learns, Daddy will be back shortly and then we'll read books and do fun stuff.

Death is not our final destiny and the Grave is not our legacy.

Objection 2. Ah, but that's easy to say and deal with philosophically. Let's see how you deal with death in reality. Let's see if that's how you feel when it happens to you.
Response: Less than five days ago[78] as I write this, my beautiful daughter Caroline Lois died in my arms. She went from her *father's* temporal arms to her *Father's* eternal arms. Her funeral was this morning. We will bury the empty frail shell of her earthly vessel in a few days. We weep for the hole she left in our hearts and our lives,

---

[77] At most, the argument moves from justifying God's actions to proving that the human actually heard from God.
[78] Dec 1st 2009 at 1:10 am.

we miss her so terribly and feel sad for ourselves, but we do not weep for *her*. We do not feel sad for *her* for the short time she had on this Earth. For she left this boring old limited world to go do what she had been designed for: *to glorify God by enjoying Him forever in all eternity.* The measly 90 years she "lost out" on *here* is nothing in comparison to eternity *there*. She went to dimensions of more colors, sounds, sights, music, tastes and relationships. She is having fun. Do not pity the dead if they know God.

Our Apologetics verifies our Theology; our Theology directs our Hopes and our Hopes guide our Emotions.

If you'd like to read the comments my wife and I made at her funeral service, please go to: **NeilMammen.WordPress.com.** We hope they will encourage you and allow you to view death with the hope of greater, better and more joyous promises rather than the despair of annihilation.

Objection 3. Why would some being spend all this time (billions of years) and energy to create this vast Universe and then put these tiny things in frail bodies in one tiny corner of the Universe while the rest of this huge Universe is all wasted?

Response: Earlier in this book I've shown the scientific and logical aspects to answering this question. Agent X is outside of time and space. So it doesn't take Agent X any "time" or "energy" to create anything. These facts make the question itself meaningless. Agent X can create the entire Universe from nothing. He creates energy from nothing; He has no shortage of it. The question comes from a human being's point of view, which is a rather constricted point of view if you think about it. "Think outside the box."

But let's assume you want to argue: If Agent X really existed, then He wouldn't have spent 9B years preparing the entire Universe before introducing planet Earth and then another 4B years before introducing man *even* if it wasn't "any effort."

First we must realize that this question presumes that there is no other intelligent life in this universe. That's quite a presumption. Atheists, especially must believe that if accidental life and random evolutionary improvements are possible, it should be happening in billions of places simultaneously. Thus they can't logically justify Earth being the *only* source of intelligent life. Christians have no such limitations. The Bible talks of multiple other types of intelligent beings. So first of all, why do you think Agent X did this only for us? We could be in a Universe teaming with life.

Second, that conclusion is false even from a "only humans exist" viewpoint. Think of your wedding, if you are married. If you aren't, think of weddings in general. How long is the actual wedding? Some of you may say, "For the rest of your life." No, that's the marriage. I'm talking about the wedding.

Here in the US, the wedding is usually about 4 to 8 hours long at the most, including the reception.

Yet, how long does it normally take to plan that wedding? Days? No, it takes months, usually 6-9 months. Do you spend that much time planning for a simple dinner? No. So the specialness of the event to you dictates the amount of time you spend planning it. That's like what God did. The specialness of us humans and the wedding of the Church and Christ was why He spent eons of "Universe Time" getting ready for it. But, guess what, like the marriage follows the wedding and lasts for a long time, the marriage of Christ to his Church lasts for all eternity. Surely, that's a worthy thing to plan for.

What's even more interesting is as Hugh Ross shows in his book, *Why the Universe is the way it is,* everything in the Universe actually has a purpose; it is there because there is no other way to create a universe that supports life like ours. That stuff is out there because God wanted to create a mechanically correct, physically sound, logical and rationally functioning planet for man to live on. Read the book to understand more of this excellent argument from an astrophysicist. www.Reasons.org.

A friend at work asked, "But why not just say 'poof' and have everything show up in an instant? If God is really omnipotent, surely he could do that." To that I asked, "What if you had gone to the great painter Matisse and told him, 'Here's a new futuristic computer. You can press this key and poof it takes a picture and then poof a new painting shows up exactly as you want it and then poof this printer here prints it out with real paint.'"

As long as he painted for his enjoyment and not for profit, what do you think Matisse would say? Do you think he'd want to do it that way? Absolutely not! If it's worth doing, it's worth taking the "effort."

Agent X is an artist.[79] He enjoys creating. He enjoys doing

---

[79] I'm not merely anthropomorphizing. Does God have a will? Yes. Does man have a will? Yes. Does God have desires? Yes. Does man have desires? Yes. If Christianity is true, one of its basic tenets is that we share certain natures with God, like our creative nature. It fits

grandiose things. Not because He has to, but because He *wants* to! Just like when you may want to do a painting, not because you need to, but because you desire to.

You see, even if creation *were* an effort (in thought and not in resources), God would enjoy the effort and may well do it for His good pleasure. After all, He is the Supreme Hedonist (as John Piper discusses in his book, *The Pleasures of God*). Just like many of *us* enjoy designing things, God may enjoy designing things. We see that in the amazing variations in creation. We all enjoy effort that is in line with our passions. I enjoyed the effort of writing this book. I didn't need to do it; I wanted to do it.

In my profession, I love the effort of designing a good board or FPGA or network processor. I enjoy it. I make sure it looks "pretty" and elegant, even though many times no one cares how pretty the schematics or elegant the RTL code is. Great painters like Matisse enjoyed every single brush stroke. My mother enjoys working hard, cooking the greatest chicken curry this world has ever known and then it pleases her to watch me enjoy it, (and just as applicable, she enjoys it even though the amount of time I take to eat it is far less than the amount of time she took to make it).

God is an artist, the very *first* artist, the mold on which all artists are made. What makes you think His doing what He loves *for* someone He loves, would be something He'd ever shirk from? He enjoys watching *you* enjoy His world that He created for you, and He'll enjoy watching you enjoy the New World, once He creates that, too.

And as my dedication to this book implies, once you've had a child, you may actually understand in some small part, why a father or mother would want to expend effort to do such grandiose things for a child who may never comprehend the extent of the things their earthly parent does for them. I think of my daughter's nursery that my wife spent months on. If that is true for us, how much more would an infinite Father do for us?[80]

---

the concepts; it's consistent, and unless you can explain why our explanation doesn't follow logically, you have to grant it validity. It does not have to be the perfect explanation; it just has to be one *possible* explanation. When dealing with a free will intelligent agent like a God or a human, unless you can show that it contradicts their very nature, you have to allow that it may well be accurate.

[80] One more thought: it is also possible that God fine-tuned every event right from the start, i.e., set all the variables precisely so that he could push the button and just sit back and watch the entire Rube Goldberg machine click away till it was ready for Him to place

The late Christopher Hitchens just couldn't seem to grasp these simple concepts as he kept asking this same question over and over again in various debates. Was it incompetence or disingenuousness? You tell me.

Objection 4. What sort of silly design is this anyway? Our galaxy is colliding with another galaxy, our sun will go nova, and everything is going to fall apart in a few billion years. This reeks of incompetence, not Omniscience.

Response: I tracked this objection down to an atheist blindly parroting Christopher Hitchens. Hitchens, who didn't even have a degree in physics, let alone astrophysics, presumed to be omniscient about the requirements for creating a universe. Worse for him, he condemned a working design at the top of his voice.

After planning for months, do you buy decorations for your wedding reception that will last 200 years? Or, do you buy quality decorations that will serve the purpose for the short time you need it? Do you buy plastic flowers that will last forever, or fresh flowers that will die after you are done with them? As for galaxies colliding, Hugh Ross explains that unless our galaxy can absorb smallish dwarf galaxies once every half a billion years, its spiral structure would have collapsed by now.[81] That structure is critical to being able to harbor advanced life on Earth. Yet arch-skeptic Hitchens apparently forgot that the Bible foretold the "wrapping up" and destruction of the Universe and our "heavens" 4,000 years ago. It is part of the very theology of the Gospel of Salvation when God will renew all things. Yet, up to 80 years ago, Hitchens' uninformed predecessor priests of atheism believed in a Universe that was eternal. At least have the integrity to admit that the Bible got it right 4,000 years before you did. You can't have it both ways.

Objection 5. But you are coming to this conclusion too early. Science may prove different things to us in the years to come.

Response: I have heard this objection many times, usually from educated people, but truly this objection shows a lack of understanding of the core of this argument. The argument I have stated is *not just* a scientific one. Please be very clear about this. It

---

man into it. The only difference is that when it was done executing, it would maintain its prescribed behavior long enough for God to accomplish His purposes.

[81] Hugh Ross, *Why The Universe Is The Way It Is*, (Grand Rapids, MI: Baker Books, 2008), 73.

uses science, but it's not a purely scientific one, it's a *logical and rational* one. Science uses logic and rationality – they are the parents of science. Let me explain.

Science is not the fundamental basis for our understanding of the way mechanistic objects act. Logic and reason are. Remember, logic and reason existed before the Universe came into being. They transcend all physical reality and existence. The arithmetic relationship 1+1 = 2 was true *before* the Big Bang and will continue to be true even *after* this and/or all universes die a heat death. There is no need of a physical universe or even a physical reality for 1+1 = 2. The concept is transcendent and eternal, similarly for logic and reasoning (at least far as human beings can ever know).

Remember, no amount of new scientific evidence will be able to change the logic that an infinitely existing mechanistic object can only do one thing in eternity past or do the same thing infinite times. (See Chapter 3.) Thus only new facts that completely refute our current measurements and scientists' analysis could change the facts that the logic is based on.

Furthermore, on this point the only discoveries that would be relevant would be things like finding actual infinite universes or evidence that the Universe is in fact eternal (i.e., evidence proving the Big Bang never happened). So are you sure you want to "wait and hope and wish" for that day to come? Perhaps you can start a religion based on that (sorry, sorry, that was just too tempting). Note that just showing that infinite universes or a single infinitely cycling universe is *possible* does not help you. God is possible too.

Remember too, that any number of *finite* multiple universes won't work. You have to have *infinite* multiple universes. Finite other universes still means that God exists because you need a non-mechanistic agent. The deck, the logic and the evidence, is stacked against the atheist.

There is no other option. And since currently the ideas of infinite universes existing, cyclical universes happening, etc., have been disproved or are un-provable or require us to blindly believe that there are billions of identical copies of you and me out there, (see Objection 7 below), all these ideas would have to be accepted on blind faith. Compare this to the idea of an intelligent, free will Agent X who has crafted a universe that specifically allows us to discover Him, which logically proceeds from the facts. I'd say *I* don't have enough faith to be an atheist. It's almost like asking me, "What if one day we find out that the Earth is really flat, we should wait for that, before coming to a conclusion?" *Really?* I just have trouble taking that seriously.

Moreover, this "waiting for future scientific discoveries" sort of argument will hurt the atheist more than it hurts the theist. After all, I can then just turn around and say: "well, you are coming to atheism too early. Maybe one day science will prove that evolution is completely false. Why aren't you waiting for *that* day before making a decision?" The concept of God predates philosophical atheism, so why not hang on to the older idea and wait. As I've said before, it's not as if I gave you a faulty argument that you are able to refute rationally. I gave you a logical argument that fits the facts. You just don't *like* the facts, so you reject the rational conclusion and beg to wait longer. But since when did liking or not liking a fact or a conclusion validate the conclusion? In science, one's personal preferences are irrelevant to the truth. Actually, they are always irrelevant when judging what objective truth.

I could be wrong, and I'm willing to be corrected, but you'd better have some real evidence and reasoning, not just a worry about the consequences of there being a God or the fact that you do not prefer what He has done in history. We don't get to vote. God's existence is not a democratic process.

Objection 6. You said that the only two options for a mechanistic thing were to do something once or do something infinite times. Why can't a third option be to do something 10 Million times and then stop (i.e., n times). This could bring us to 13.7B years.

Response: Actually, this question misunderstands the concept and reflects confusion about subtracting anything from infinity. Even if a mechanistic thing does something 10 million times, in eternity past those 10 million times will have already transpired long before 13.7B years ago. In other words: Infinity minus (10M multiplied by any value of time) is still infinity.

Or you can think of those 10 million events as one group of events. That group of events must have occurred in eternity past. Thus, there is again no basis for thinking that a mechanistic thing could do something at a certain point in time that is not eternally ancient. (See ahead for the "timeless" objection).

Objection 7. Couldn't the same[82] singularity indeed be mechanistically creating infinite multiple universes?

Response: As discussed in this book the answer is: Yes, multiple infinite universes are certainly a possibility and would feasibly explain how we don't need a God. But there are some major problems with this.

  A. There is no evidence for infinite universes and having just a few other universes is not sufficient; with any mechanistic first cause you have to have infinite universes.[83]

  B. You cannot falsify the infinite universe theory, so it's certainly not scientific. You *can* falsify the Big Bang Theory and many of our other conclusions.

  C. Currently, we have no mechanism to explain why or how one singularity could give rise to infinite universes. Science currently can and does only show one and only one Big Bang for our singularity. If you were going to suggest Loop Quantum Cosmology then you have other problems. I'll deal with this in a later objection.

  D. We would need to explain why one universe would never have any effect on another universe created by the same singularity. For example, how could one singularity give rise to infinite universes, especially infinite universes that do not intersect in *any* way despite having a common source? Not that it is impossible, but one would wish that a viable mechanism would be presented.

  E. Given the much higher chances that it's more likely that intelligent life would evolve on planet that did *not* lend itself to discovery (because there's no correlation between life and ease of discovery), why did we somehow, accidently, amazingly end up in one of those universes where our planet is *also* designed for discovery? This means there is another you and me out there in a Universe and we were not able to discover anything about the Big Bang. Wow, that's convenient isn't it that we are on this one? I have to tell you I just don't have that much blind faith.

---

[82] If there are multiple singularities (rather than one), then what caused them and why did they not all mechanistically create the Universe in infinity past – putting us back to the same problem as before: Why *only* 13.7B years ago and not longer? The only way this question above becomes valid is if a single singularity was constantly and mechanistically creating multiple universes from infinity past. This would then be a possible feasible answer as to why our universe was only created 13.7B years ago.

[83] Note I'd actually argue that we could have at least 3 universes in the Christian view. But you need an Infiniverse for the Atheist view.

F. You can't smell them, taste them, hear them, calculate them, feel them, see them, sense them, or interact with them. Isn't that the argument you had against God? Why the sudden change in standards?

G. The only thing justifying this belief it seems is the distaste for an intelligent Agent X. In other words, could it be that you only suggest this and adhere to it because you don't *like* the other option. Not because you can prove the other option is invalid. I may be wrong but it sure smells like blind faith, i.e., it's like what I tell my religious friends (including the Christians). You *want* there to be an eternal life so you believe in it without any evidence. Don't you think that you should make sure there *is* eternal life and that it is through Christ? Fortunately, for them there is ample proof if they just look at the logical, historical and rational evidence. Similarly for atheists: You don't want there to be a moral judge at the end of time nor do you want to kowtow to anyone's rules or worship any God, so you believe He doesn't exist.

Now I realize I'm ascribing a motive here and I did say that if the facts were there then the motivation behind the argument is not relevant. But here's why this is different. The facts are *not* there to support an unbelievable infinitude of your and my universes. The facts point to an opposite conclusion. Thus, we are analyzing the motivation of a person who believes in the face of opposing facts, and that is a valid endeavor.

So, while someone is free to believe in infinite universes with every possible scenario existing, it would be based on *pure blind* faith not a *rational* faith. In other words, it would be a fantastic belief based on the absence of any evidence rather than the presence of any evidence. After all as we've noted, the atheist cannot see, touch, taste, smell, interact, or see the effects of these alternative universes. So if the atheist wants to believe this, then he should admit that he believes this without any factual basis, just a romantic notion that's a weaker notion than the concept than there are no infinite universes. He may as well believe in Pink Floating Elephant gods who are invisible and carry the globe on their back. We can't see them because they are invisible and can't be measured.

Meanwhile as we've shown, the alternative theory of a Free Will Non-Mechanistic Extra-Dimensional Agent is a much more rational and scientific theory.

Further responses in this section will deal with this in even more detail.

Objection 8. **(Taken from a book review on Amazon) In this excellent book, NASA physicist Carlos Calle tackles the question of whether the Universe requires a supernatural "designer" or whether our cosmological theories can explain the wondrous reality around us.**

The standard model of cosmology, in which a tiny piece of inflating "false vacuum" decays into a fireball, and stars and galaxies congeal out of the cooling debris, has passed many tests, but problems remain. Where did the false vacuum come from in the first place? And how do the supposedly enormous quantum convulsions of our current vacuum manage to cancel out to almost - but not exactly - zero, leaving behind a piddling "dark energy" that lies in the tiny range of values that allow life to exist?

Physics and cosmology alone may have the answers, says Calle. Combine eternal inflation, in which the primordial false vacuum continuously grows and decays, with string theory and you end up with a multiverse - a vast collection of universes, each of which has a different amount of dark energy. We find ourselves in one where it has just the right value for stars, planets, and life because... well, we couldn't find ourselves anywhere else.

Another cosmological model that has emerged from string theory has our Universe living on the surface of a "brane" floating in a higher-dimensional space. Our brane collides with a nearby brane over and over again for eternity, triggering an endless sequence of Big Bangs. This cyclic model may home in on the exact value of the dark energy we measure.

The model doesn't require a beginning, and some theorists suspect that eternal inflation may not either. Certainly, neither requires a designer. Cosmology still has a lot to figure out, Calle contends, but it is in good shape.

To which a couple of commenters said:

A: *I hope the book explains why a self-existent, infinite Universe (or "multiverse" to use the fashionable term) is more believable than a self-existent infinite god.*

B: *I can of course not hope to have an explanation for how anything at all could possibly be infinite or eternal, but the self-*

existent, infinite Universe has a slight advantage that makes it less unbelievable than a self-existent, infinite God: we can observe it. No reliable observations of God have been made so far. Thus, worshipping the Universe makes actually more sense than worshipping God, if any worshipping needs to be done.

Response: Hopefully the reader has seen the problem in the "commenters" and in Calle's claims. Note too that there are many astronomers out there (even atheists) who are just as educated as Calle and who **reject** his conclusions.

1. Any time Calle postulates a source, i.e., Branes or quantum convulsions or quantum fluctuations or a vacuum that grows and decays or some other cause, we must recall: "Non-Mechanistic First Cause." (See Chapter 3 above.) And these speculated causes are **not** nothing. They are something. Remember the Big Bang Theory claims that the cause of the Big Bang is timeless, spaceless and energy-less. That kind of cause is *not* a vacuum fluctuation. You can't even have a vacuum without space and you can't have a fluctuation without time.

Any of these speculated causes would have to fulfill all the requirements of the "spinning top" example, which they can *only* do if there exist an infinite number of universes.

2. So Calle, realizing the problem, has to fall back on multiverses and infinite universes. As that's the *only* way to explain our fine-tuned universe. But he also realizes that he cannot prove these infinite universes, so he falls back on saying something like "we still have a lot to figure out but we are in good shape." He also says his theories are more reasonable than a theory of God.

What's funny is that the commenter says: *No reliable observations of God have been made so far.*

Ah seriously? Did you consider that no reliable observations of the Infini-verse have been made either?

Calle's argument ends up being Science of the Gaps, i.e., our science leads us to two conclusions (God or infinite universes) so we'll just take the more improbable one because we don't like the moral consequences of the other and we'll hope and wait for the evidence. Yet the opposite is the more logical conclusion. We have to go with what science and common sense reasoning tells us is the more reasonable of the two.

Ah, but you say: How is God the less improbable one? Why is the God postulate more probable? For that, read the response to this next objection, which builds on previous objections.

Objection 9.But multiple universes blow your entire argument to bits. Or: All you've done is show that multiple universes are just as likely as the existence of God or the Free willed Agent. I think it's easier to believe in a multiverse.

Response: As I noted, yes, there are only 2 options:

1. A free willed personal non-mechanistic Agent X, or
2. Infinite universes.

First, let's clarify the problems with the Infiniverse theories. Note I'm not talking about one or two alternate universes (I actually think there may well be 2 others and we may even end up being able to detect them). I'm talking about the Infiniverse.

Any theory of infinite alternative universes you propose has this *major* set of problems:

You can't touch them.

You can't smell them.

You can't taste them.

You can't feel them.

You can't see them.

You can't measure them.

You can't calculate their existence.

You can't make any verifiable predictions of them.

You can't electro-magnetically, gravitationally or using sonar, sense them.

You can't interact with them. You can make predictions but you can't verify any of those predictions.

And unlike the multiple dimensions of the Universe that we also don't see but *can indeed* calculate, we can't calculate or derive any actual details or characteristics of these infinite universes. True, you can postulate some nice-to-have features, but you cannot derive any actual details. In fact, you could postulate anything about these universes and it would be impossible to falsify it. Note the nature of the God that we've deduced in this book is not so vague and speculative.

And before we stop, remember: the existence of one other universe is not sufficient to overcome the problems that the multiverse theories have. There *have* to be infinite other universes. A million universes is too little, a billion doesn't work either. You need infinite universes.

Why? Because even if it takes 300B years (whatever that means outside of time) to form one universe, a non-mechanistic agent acting *from eternity* would have had enough "time" to make infinite universes. Any non-mechanistic agent inside or outside of time has to give us infinite universes and it will start to make those universes in "no time."

What's worse, the Multi-Universe theory is not scientific.
Why do I say that? Especially when many scientists postulate it? As stated before, we can't falsify it. That alone doesn't disprove it, but it sure makes it suspect and we'd need very good reasons to believe it. It's very similar to what my atheist friends claim about God. So I must ask, can you show me a test that would falsify the multiverse theory? There is none that we know of currently that we can actually do scientifically. So therefore, the multiverse theory is currently quite unscientific. If you believe it, you have to believe it on faith in the lack of any evidence. Are you sure that to a super skeptic rational free thinker like me you really wish to posit an unscientific *belief* as your best argument? You'd have a lot more guts than I do to try to stand on this fact. Especially as this belief may have some serious long-term consequences.

So you have to admit without any evidence one must *blindly* believe the multiverse exists. If you really are like me, demanding a thing be proven to be reasonable before you will believe it, then surely you can see why I think blindly believing in multiverses is a bit too "religious" for me. It's almost fanatical. It's like some cult leader telling their followers that the Comet Hale-Bopp has a spaceship hiding behind it that you can't see, touch, taste, smell, hear, measure, or falsify the existence of. "But believe you me...it is there. Now go put on your Nike's and track suits and then drink this poison so we can get on board." Sorry man, but I am not a cool-aid drinker. I want to see evidence. I hope you understand my skepticism. Don't feel singled out; I approach Christianity the same way.

Here's another problem. The huge weakness of multiverse theory is akin to what atheists have been complaining about for centuries about God. They say: "Hey, you can't touch, smell, taste, feel, see, or interact with God. So therefore, God doesn't exist." But here in one swell foop (okay, one fell swoop), they say, "Hey we don't believe in God for these reasons... but trust me: Infinite Universes really really do exist. I can't prove it. But trust me blindly, using the same reasons that I used to reject belief in God. *You* have to have faith in those infinite universes." Why the sudden change in standards?

Let me share this personal experience. Ignacio Reyes, a

friend of mine, is a young college student and one of the San Jose Live Action leaders. Live Action is a team of students who go undercover to expose abortion providers like Planned Parenthood and show that they are violating the law by not reporting statutory rape. (Go to www.liveactionfilms.org to see these secret camera stings). Ignacio arranged for a debate with an atheist friend of his. At the last minute, his atheist friend chickened out of the debate. Ignacio asked me to help find him a substitute. I suggested he visit the Silicon Valley Atheist's website and see if they could connect him with an atheist student. Ignacio did so and the president of the Silicon Valley Atheists said he'd debate Ignacio. I was worried about this young college kid debating a hardened atheist. I hadn't meant for him to debate the *president* of the group. I thought the atheists would have been gracious and found him some other student instead of having him go head to head with a veteran 55-year old.

I needn't have worried. Ignacio destroyed him in the debate[84] using material similar to what's in this book. Part way through the Q&A from the audience, the president of the atheists said, "You *have* to believe there are multiple universes. I know you can't see them, but they are there. You just have to believe me."

The crowd erupted in laughter. Doesn't that sound like a blind faith Christian or religious fanatic? It seemed like the president of the local atheists was spouting his faith-based testimony.

When we add the point that the Earth seems designed for discovery, you have compound problems. First, you *need* infinite universes, some of which allow life to evolve just so. Second, *you* need to coincidentally be in one of the universes where Earth ended up designed perfectly for discovery. The coincidences are just a bit too fantastic. [85]

If there are infinite universes, then you are postulating that in many of those universes, the planet where intelligent life exists is *not* designed for discovery. But there are other problems with infinite

---

[84] We conducted a write-in poll beforehand of the entire audience and asked who were atheists, agnostics, or theists of any kind. We polled the audience again just prior to dismissing the group, asking which debater had the best argument. Predictably, all the atheists thought the atheist had won and all the theists thought Ignacio had won. However, a number of the agnostics voted for Ignacio as having the best argument. In other words, the folks who were open to either possibility voted with the theist.

[85] Yes, the one universe would be a subset of the infinite universes, but there would still be an infinite number of them. But we just "happened" to be on one of those. When does the fantastic-ness of this all become a bit too "fairy-tailish" for you to buy?

universes (remember again: I actually think there may well be multiple universes, but for this to work you have to have *infinite* universes, not just multiple universes, because the option of having a *few* other universes defeats your mechanistic position – it has to be infinite in number).

Moreover, if there are infinite universes then by necessity there are universes where Earth exists but every alternative option has been taken. Every alternative and possible event has occurred. For instance, in any given situation there has to be a world where when certain persons predicts the future it always comes to pass, another where a single person wins every single lottery. Yet another where any time anybody randomly picks a card from a deck, it is *always* the ace of spades regardless of how many times the deck has been fairly shuffled or how many times it has been tried. In that kind of universe, scientists might believe the laws of probability do not exist for this event, because they are in the one universe where the probability is the same as in our Universe but a highly improbable event keeps recurring over and over again. And they have no way to explain the recurring improbable event even if they study the problem for a billion years.

In the infinite universe view, there is another universe where anytime someone tosses a coin it always comes up heads. Even when they make a machine to toss coins and see what comes up and they do it a billion times, the coin always comes up heads. Remember we are dealing with infinite multiple universes. **So, that means the probability is 1 that any physically possible scenario that we can envision would be true multiple times somewhere in some universe.**[86]

Are you having as much trouble as I in believing this? It is necessary that for every decision you made, there is an alternative universe that evolved in the exact same way except at the point of your decision, the "you" in the other universe picked one of the other myriad of choices and thus differs in only that way. It gets even more fantastical as you think on it more.

As Tim Keller so wisely says: Imagine we are playing Poker and my hand always comes up aces, you then turn to me and say, "You are cheating." I say, "Oh no, we are just in that universe where

---

[86] And it would not depend on chance, because there would be infinite chances for it to have occurred. In other words every chance would have occurred multiple times.

Neil Mammen

I always come up aces." Would you be so gullible as to believe this? Or would you say, "Do you think I'm an idiot? You are cheating."

So then why are you asking me to believe that nonsensical improbability when it comes to universes? Would you accept the "this universe always gives me aces" answer? Of course, you wouldn't. You'd be an absolute idiot to accept it, a sucker. Then why would you accept the nonsensical improbability when it comes to the multiverse theory? Is it that you are so afraid of, or so hate the idea of a supreme Agent X that you reject logic for a superstitious fairy tale?

Infinite quantum universes have even more insidious consequences. The Quantum Universe theory (based on an initial infinitely-old universe) is where for every choice you make a new universe is spawned where the other "you" takes the other option or options. In that theory, no one can say that any act is evil or should not be committed. Why not? Because the Quantum Universe theorist would respond (for example): "Well, we just happen to be in those universes where Hitler decided to kill the Jews, if it hadn't happened in this universe, it would have happened in another one. So, what's the big difference, it was bound to happen." Free will, it seems, goes out the door. Morality goes out the door.

In fact, with infinite universes, there have to be almost infinite exact duplicates of this very universe where we are doing the exact same thing as well. There are redundant copies of you and me.

Now you may object, "But each attempt of a universe is a new attempt, (like each time you throw the dice you still have a one in six chance of rolling say, a three), so there's no likelihood that we would have any duplicates."

But that would be an invalid claim, because first, if you take a 6-faced die and toss it 600 times, statistically you'd expect to see a normal distribution, i.e., you'd expect to see a three about 100 times or so. If you got only 1 three, you'd start to suspect that the die was being controlled or had been designed or mis-designed to disfavor the three (which would support the non-mechanistic agent concept, since you can't get a mis-design without a designer). It would be irrational and unscientific to think that despite the random chances, you would never get more than 1 three without a free-willed Agent.

Similarly you'd have to explain, despite the normal distribution, what the chances are that we'd have just one and only one such universe with such a perfectly fine tuned Earth that *also* seems designed for discovery (remember there is no "need" for our Earth to be designed for discovery) for life to exist. You'd need a few trillion billion such worlds that slightly differ and *weren't* designed for discovery yet had intelligent life just to get one that *was* designed for discovery. Thus the atheist has to argue that there are trillions of similar worlds that are just slightly different. So why not trillions of similar worlds that are identical except for the Poker game results? Why should we stop at it being designed for discovery?

You may also object saying, "But the chances of a Royal Flush in each universe are just as rare, so of course I'd be suspicious." But this again hurts your case, because then why are you not suspicious of the 37 fine tuning points which are more incredibly rare than 37 Royal Flushes?

In addition if there are truly infinite universes, then there would be universes where though the mathematical probability of a Royal Flush is the same as anywhere (0.00000153908), whenever we play Poker using a fairly shuffled card deck, I always get Royal Flushes. Why? Because with infinite universes each with slight variations needed to get fine-tuned Big Bangs, the standard distribution should result in one or more universes where all my ducks simply line up in a row. It's the "Royal Flush" universe and we are in it. Why don't you buy it?

Moreover, who is the supreme intellect monkeying with the variables and keeping them constant across the universes? Why don't we get a normal distribution? In some universes you should get 1 royal flush in a row, in others 2 and in yet others 10. Why do you complain?

But now consider: isn't this the same argument atheists have used to argue how life came into existence? That there were billions of accidental tries until a few worked? And your argument is that with billions of years and tries we'd eventually get life and billions more tries and we get Britney Spears freebasing. Why doesn't your Royal Flush objection work here? Remember just one instance of non-living materials accidentally morphing into a living organism would not be sufficient, because that organism could have died on the spot or gotten destroyed by some inorganic event (like a lava eruption).[87] You can't say all the tries were related. Perhaps additional mutations were dependent, but the first ones were not. So you are stuck with infinite me's and you's out there, some playing Poker and none of them questioning the improbability of the same player getting a Royal Flush every hand.

Now you may be tempted to say, "Ah, but then we are on equal ground. You can't prove God exists and I can't prove infinite universes exist."[88]

But, I think that's where you may not realize there are yet unelaborated points of this issue. There are at least six other weighty arguments for the existence of God. Of the two options, i.e., infinite universes or an infinite being, these arguments show the God hypothesis is the more plausible one based on the evidence.

1. The Impossibility Argument

Taking the most critical position, mechanistic abiogenesis (i.e., life from non-life) is impossible. At best, mechanistic abiogenesis is unscientific because it is not repeatable or provable or falsifiable. Yet, atheists must *irrationally* insist it is possible even though we can scientifically prove that it never happens naturally. Even the Miller-Urey experiment which some tried to claim proved that abiogenesis could occur given an electric spark, has been discredited as not being performed in the likely pre-life atmosphere of the Earth, and even when given the skewed enhanced beginnings, that experiment didn't create life, it merely created amino acids. Of course, as we now know, saying that amino acids are equivalent to life is as ignorant as when Darwin thought that living cells were merely some globs of protoplasm when in fact they are huge complex biochemical factories.

2. The Moral Argument

If Objective Moral values exist, then God exists. Objective Moral values *do* exist, thus God exists.

See *www.WilliamLaneCraig.com* for the argument for this.

3. The Christological and Historical Argument.

There is good historical evidence for the authenticity of the New

---

[87] See Lee M. Spetner, *Not by Chance!: Shattering the Modern Theory of Evolution*, (Brooklyn, NY: Judaica Press, 1998), 54-57.

[88] Don't forget too that even if Infiniverses did exist, that would not prove that God does not exist. It only seems to indicate that we "don't" need a first cause to explain the Universe. This is not proof positive that *no* God exists.

Testament gospels. The gospels and history give good evidence that Jesus Christ is God. This includes evidence for Jesus' physical resurrection. Remember, if Agent X exists, then His raising someone from the dead is trivial. See *www.WilliamLaneCraig.com* again for the argument on this. This argument may sound like the weakest one here, but in reality, it is one of the strongest ones, once you look at the facts and the logic.

4. The Improbability of Evolution Argument

Atheists posit that the evolution of life by undirected mutation and natural selection happened, despite steep odds against it. For example, evolutionist Julian Huxley said in his book *Evolution in Action:*[89]

> The odds of getting a number of favorable mutations in one strain through pure chance alone are: A thousand to a millionth power, when written out, that becomes the figure 1 with 3 million zeros after it; ... No one would bet on anything so improbable happening. And yet it has happened! It has happened thanks to the working of natural selection and the properties of living substance which make natural selection inevitable!

Note that there are only 10^{82} atoms in the entire Universe[90] and Huxley is proposing that the chance for a single speciation is 1 in $10^{3,000,000}$ (when one species evolves into another). Do you realize Huxley was estimating a probability so small that you'd have to throw the "dice" on every atom in the Universe simultaneously for gazillions of years before getting the possibility of one speciation? Yet an atheist has to irrationally believe that, or prove Huxley wrong. No wonder many atheists cling to the infinite multiverse theory for evolution, too. That way they can say the evolution of any one species only works *once* for every $10^{2,999,760}$ Universes,[91] but at least it works. With infinite universes, the vast improbability of evolution isn't a problem. Except: in fact, the infinite universes theory is a bigger problem.

I just don't have enough faith to believe in those sorts of odds. I

---

[89] Julian Huxley, *Evolution in Action,* (London: Chatto & Windus, 1953), 41. Please don't imagine that because this is an older book the odds have suddenly become better. In fact, if anything I would think the odds have become worse.

[90] http://www.universetoday.com/36302/atoms-in-the-universe/

[91] I admit, there's no real statistical correlation here, but you get the idea.

don't have enough faith to be an atheist.

5. The Intelligence Argument

All science (except for evolutionary theories) currently tells us that anything complex that looks like it was intelligently design is most probably intelligently designed.[92] Take the coding of DNA. Sure, it's hypothetically possible that it is un-designed, but how *reasonable* is it to think that it is? Talk to murder scene investigators and ask them whether they tend to assume things occur by accident at crime scenes. Only an *in*competent or corrupt CSI agent would claim that the arrangement of evidence only "looks designed but is a natural phenomenon" as the primary explanation for a homicide.

We don't function in our daily lives as though everything is the product of physical accident. Why do it when it comes to science? Science is supposed to be *more* rational, not less rational. So the atheist suffers the disadvantage of having to believe *against* common sense that things that *look* intelligently designed are *not* intelligently designed.

At what point can I take my brain back off the shelf and start using it again?

6. The issue of how the Biblical text just happens to be able to predict the Big Bang prior to science being able to tell us this.

Perhaps you'll say "*all* creation myths start that way; it's natural for everyone to want a beginning." But that is simply not true; it's only the Judeo-Christian Creation that has a transcendent extra-dimensional God who creates out of nothing. In every other culture (about which I have heard) the creation is made from pre-existing materials. Only Judeo-Christianity has a God who creates Time. All other religions don't even understand the concept of a timeless beginning.[93]

Naturally, I only introduce these points, as space does not permit providing any arguments here. For arguments, please see

---

[92] The SETI project, searching for signs of intelligent life elsewhere in the Universe, seeks to detect radio signals that carry patterns that appear the product of intelligence. Why do we imagine that is designed but DNA is not? Is it because DNA can "evolve" into more complicated things? But where did it get that ability to do that? Was that ability to evolve designed?

[93] Not even Chronos did, as he existed in Time already with his Father Uranus. A "non-theistic" 12-year old provided this rebuttal while I was showing his atheistic father this presentation.

www.NoBlindFaith.com or email us and we'll send you write-ups on them or refer you to William Lane Craig's or others' arguments.

You might insist that if we had infinite universes then even all of these improbabilities could feasibly have happened randomly. But go back to the Poker example that we discussed previously: I am playing Poker with you and I keep coming up with a Royal Flush every hand, you challenge me about that, and I say, "Look, pal, we just happen to be in one of those many universes where I always come up with a Royal Flush." Are you going to accept that answer? I hope you see the silliness of this. More rationally, you are going to suspect someone stacked the deck or is controlling the cards. At some point, reality needs to kick in – you don't live your life as though reality is randomly flexible. We would not want our governments or police to operate that way either.

Certainly you are free to disagree with any of these six points, but if you are a thinking person you should at least give them skeptical due diligence. No single one of them proves that God exists without any doubt, but viewing them all together it becomes more reasonable to believe that a God exists than to have *blind* faith that infinite universes exist despite the impossibility of proving that view rationally. In other words, there is more rational weight on the side that some sort of intelligent agent exists than on the side that an Infiniverse exists. I don't expect you to accept this instantly, but I hope you at least see that the overwhelming evidence seems to be on the intelligent agent side.

And we still have the logically robust Agent X argument that can be summarized as:

The first cause has to be eternal, powerful enough to create a universe, non-mechanistic, free-willed, extra-dimensional, personal enough to want us to discover Him and knowledgeable enough to create a fine-tuned universe.

At the least, you have to admit that you are forced to have as much blind faith in infinite universes as a theist in an unknown God. At which point Blaise Pascal's premise starts to make good sense. He believed it wise to avoid the path of the most disadvantage. The traditional atheist's responses to Pascal cannot stand against the reasoning we apply here.[94]

---

[94] Pascal said: "Either God exists or He doesn't. Either I believe in God or I don't. Of the four possibilities, only one is to my disadvantage. To avoid that possibility, I believe in God." Quoted in Des MacHale, *Wisdom* (London, 2002).

As an added resource on this issue, I recommend the book *Who's afraid of the Multiverse?* by Jeffrey Zweerink (Reasons to Believe, 2008).[95]

Objection 10. Why do we need infinite universes, when we could just have had infinite Big Bangs and only one of them worked?

Response: Actually this argument contains a false premise. If you have infinite Big Bangs, then it would take a lot of blind faith to believe that only one single Big Bang was successful in creating a universe that was just right for solid matter, just right for life and just right for discovery. Infinite Big Bangs, each with minor differences (to yield one with the precise fine-tuned mix), will lead to infinite universes where you and I evolved in almost identical ways with only minor differences. Any possible scenario must have been actualized in one or more of those Big Bangs – anything else is irrational because of the definition of "infinite."

Objection 11. But you wouldn't get duplicates of us because there are infinite possibilities of things that could happen.

Response: This argument comes from the fallacious assumption that the number of combinations of events in any universe is infinite. But this is simply not true. Given any finite universe, the number of possible combinations of events in *that* universe will never be *infinite*. It will be huge, but *finite*. Thus in eternity which *is* infinite, if you have more than one universe with the same starting conditions, then it seems logical there will inevitably be duplicate

---

In other words; if I don't believe in God and God *does* exist as described, then I go to Hell, but if there is no god then it's not a big deal. So why take a chance? Hell is a lousy option.

Pascal's approach makes sense if you have come to a fork in the road based on the information and *have* to choose one path. I'm suggesting that you have.

We should also take the time to refute some standard atheist responses to Pascal. For instance "Well, why not say the same about worshiping the pink unicorn, better believe in him lest you go to unicorn hell?" Here's the answer to that sarcastic challenge: There aren't six powerful arguments similar to those presented above that support the existence of a divine pink unicorn. If there was a stronger argument for the pink unicorn than for God, then you should go for it. It'd be stupid not to.

Other common atheist arguments fail the same way. For examples, atheists have mocked the arguments by saying: (1) "I should believe in *all* the gods, and myths, just in case one of them is right;" or (2) "what if there's a god that says 'if you *do* believe in me you go to hell', then I'd really be screwed." These objections fail similarly because there are no rational arguments supporting: (1) those myths and gods, or logic that supports (2) the cosmic "Hell if you believe in me" god. We are rational thinking people. Go where the evidence leads. It is of no value and actually hypocritical to be an irrational atheist.

[95] Available at www.reasons.org

universes. You might counter by suggesting each *type* of universe could have infinite possibilities and each universe is completely independent of each other so each universe spawns its own huge combination of possibilities. But remember, the very reason that the Infiniverse was grasped so eagerly by people like Dr. Laurence Krauss was because it gave him a way to explain the fine tuning of the Universe without needing God. Krauss et al say that given infinite universes that are slightly different from each other, inevitably it will result in one (or more) with the perfect fine tuning like our universe. If you now say that each universe is independent from each other then the "gradually getting a fine-tuned Universe" excuse goes out the door and you are back, stuck with an intelligent omniscient designer.

Postulating universes that all start by different causes and are not related to each other raises more problems. If any set of universes is caused by any *one* mechanistic process, then those possibilities are not infinite. It does not rescue your argument to say the universes are being started by infinite different processes, because we only care about the universes that are started by the same process that started *our* universe. Remember, we only need a *single* eternally old mechanistic Agent X to result in infinite universes. Thus we come back to a finite number of variants and over eternity this will be repeated.

If you cling to the non-duplicating Infiniverse contention, then actually your argument is not with me, but with atheist cosmologists and physicists like Vilenkin, Weinberg and Carr as well as *New Scientist* magazine editors like Amanda Gefter. They all contend that multiple duplicate universes exist with slight variations of each other.

Objection 12. What about Loop Quantum Cosmology/Gravity theories (LQC)?

Response: LQC, promoted heavily by Abhay Ashtekar, is really just a variation of the infinite universes idea but asserts a single cyclically rebounding universe. It's a way to try to resolve the fact that we see no leftover (residual) energy after a universe has contracted and "restarted." But consider three things about LQC. First, we can't verify the theory. Second, there is nothing in theory that says that infinite recycling is required. It is hypothetically possible, i.e., it's one possible solution, but it cannot really be verified using the scientific method. There are no predictions that are solely explainable by LQC theory.[96] Third, the Achilles' heel of this theory is that it is decimated by the Borde-Guth-Vilenkin theorem.[97] This theorem (note, it's not a *theory* but a *theorem,* i.e., a proposition that has been proven through explicit assumptions), proves that even with a multiverse, in this case a repeating universe, there must have been a beginning, a "first" universe. Notably, this means the LQC universe can't be infinitely old. And the moment (pun intended) you have a non-eternal "anything" you need a non-mechanistic agent and you are stuck all over again with that "awful horrible" free will agent out there who just refuses to disappear due to logic and rationality. So LQC is not our savior from Agent X (pun intended).

On top of all of that, the LQC "possibility" doesn't relieve us of the embarrassing infinite universe requirement. For LQC to eliminate this terribly hated non-mechanistic agent, we still have to believe in infinite universes, but in this case they just happen to be sequential not parallel. So, we are still stuck with the fact that somewhere in the past, every possible variation of this universe has already taken place (rather than happening concurrently).

Think of it as a sequentially infinite universe, including *infinite copies of this exact universe.* Why? Because this exact universe has to have happened in the past because there are infinite universes in the past, and it will happen again because there are infinite universes in the future. So "you" have already read this statement infinite times before and you will do it infinite times again. In addition, we have to believe that of all the universes out there, we "just happened" in one of the ones that was designed for discovery. Of course there are *infinite* other designed for discovery universes out there as well and in some you are the author of this book and I'm the one who is reading this. Could I say, "It's just a bit too much superstition for me? A bit too much Twilight Zonish." Sure the infinite universe idea is hypothetically possible. But is that idea more *reasonable* than positing the existence of a free will Agent X? It doesn't seem so partially because of the 6 extra arguments in favor of the non-mechanistic Agent X.

---

[96] Scientists predicted that there would be a cosmic background radiation as a result of the initial Big Bang and they later found it.

http://hyperphysics.phy-astr.gsu.edu/hbase/astro/PenWil.html

[97] Arvind Borde, Alan H. Guth, and Alexander Vilenkin, "Inflationary spacetimes are not past-complete," *Phys.Rev.Lett*, 90 (2003), DOI: 10.1103/PhysRevLett.90.151301 (accessed November 25, 2012).

Objection 13. But you've just assumed that the causality line extends to infinity past. What if the line of causation just began, then the 13.7B years old is feasible.

Response: Actually this viewpoint is not feasible either. There are two ways to refute it. First, the possibility of causality either exists or doesn't. It can't begin to exist unless "causality" itself has a cause and you are back in trouble with the mechanistic agent problem. But even then, if it has a "chance" of beginning to exist out of nothing in infinite nothingness, then why *didn't* this causality begin to exist *eternally* ago? You are merely pushing the problem back and that does not help you because you still run into the mechanistic bane of your theory.

The second problem would be: Even if I give you that it "just" began 14B years ago or a short while ago, what about the future? Won't it continue creating infinite other universes by this atemporal causality? Surely, you have no logical or scientific premise to insist that if something pops out of nothing once, it could never do it again. And thus in the eternal future, even if it had once chance in a bazillion of popping into existence, we'd end up with infinite universes and thus infinite copies of you and me playing Poker somewhere and always getting royal flushes. It ends up being an issue of asking: Is this reasonable? To me as a scientist, it just doesn't cut the mustard. But who am I to stop someone from blindly and superstitiously believing it?

And why stop there, why not believe other things blindly? Like flying spaghetti monsters, unicorns, large planet eating dragons, astrology. And of course we must ask, why not then believe in God blindly? After all, if one can without logic or evidence believe in things popping out of nothing, then surely believing in a God is an easy step. It's just a different blind faith belief, right?

One is reminded about the ancient Roman beliefs, some believed in one set of gods, others believed in another set, it was all arbitrary. Is this what atheism has become – a smorgasbord of unscientific and irrational explanations?

Objection 14. But in your example of a mechanistic Agent X, you said that if the agent was mechanistic then the Universe would be eternal. But why is this true, if there was no time before the Universe was created?

Response: Once the Universe was created, time would begin to exist. Once time existed, then the mechanistic agent would coexist alongside time and you could measure time. Thus if the Universe was created by a mechanistic agent, it would have done so whenever "outside" of time it was going to do so, but once it had done that, time would exist and we'd be able to see that the Universe was infinitely old and so was time. Maybe you were next going to raise a non-mechanistic objection, i.e., what if the agent had just decided to do it recently … whoops … mechanistic agents can't *decide*!

Okay, rephrase that: let's say the mechanistic agent had just by chance done it recently. That doesn't work either, because if the mechanistic agent were going to do it, even if the probability was 10^{-2B} it would have happened in eternity past, because again once a universe was created, time would exist and the countdown would begin. In other words, with infinite probability and infinite causality, the Universe would have occurred and time would have begun an eternity ago. You would have to come up with a reason why this causality **must** be **only** 13.7B years ago and not before. Before you reject this argument, read again this response from William Lane Craig:

> *In fact, I think that it can be plausibly argued that the cause of the Universe must be a personal Creator. For how else could a temporal effect arise from an eternal cause? If the cause were simply a mechanically operating set of necessary and sufficient conditions existing from eternity, then why would not the effect also exist from eternity? For example, if the cause of water's being frozen is the temperature's being below zero degrees, then if the temperature were below zero degrees from eternity, then any water present would be frozen from eternity. The only way to have an eternal cause but a temporal effect would seem to be if the cause is a personal agent who freely chooses to create an effect in time. For example, a man sitting from eternity may will to stand up; hence, a temporal effect may arise from an eternally existing agent. Indeed, the agent may will from eternity to create a temporal effect, so that no change in the agent need be conceived. Thus, we are brought not merely to the first cause of the Universe, but to its personal Creator.*
> *http://www.leaderu.com/truth/3truth11.html*

Objection 15. But what if we think of non-time as a line. Then any point on that line in eternity would be simultaneous with any other point. Thus whenever time began it would begin and then it would take 13.7B years for life to evolve and that life to then realize the Universe was 13.7B years old.

Response: This idea theoretically might solve the "eternality" problem that Craig discussed in the last objection, but it still does not escape the infinite universe problem. Here's why: When you add the fine tuning of the Universe, the fine tuning of Earth, the location of Earth for discovery and abiogenesis,[98] you realize that you'd need incredible faith to think that only one universe was accidently created (a sheer miracle) and it magically had all these characteristics. The only way this could work rationally is if there were infinite universes and we are one of the many of them that worked. This objection *also* doesn't work for the other arguments like the moral argument, and the resurrection argument, etc. Note you can't argue that the Universe *evolved* into a working model. The fine-tuned constants prove that the Big Bang is an all or nothing process. So you land back at "we just happened to be on *this* universe" which is merely one of infinite others where you are the atheist and I am the Christian, but in some universes, I'm the atheist and you are the Christian. Does this sound more reasonable to you? It does *not* to me!

Objection 16. What if the Singularity were eternal? Then it would just have had one Big Bang and that's when time would have begun.

Response: It's an interesting suggestion, but we know that the Singularity itself is not eternal. Why? Because we can state assuredly that science has deduced that prior to the Singularity and the Big Bang there was nothing. If the Singularity were eternal, then you couldn't have anything causally or temporally prior to it. Since we do know that prior to this, there was nothing, we logically realize the Singularity is not eternal. But to add to the argument, you are also stuck with the magical way a single Big Bang gave us the fine-tuned universe. We'd need a lot of big banging from this eternal universe to get this fine-tuned one. As a result we are back to the problems of the non-mechanistic agent.

---

[98] Not Darwinism mind you, but I can give you that for free, because it won't help you. Your goose was cooked long before Earth could be formed.

Objection 17. What about chaos theory? If the Big Bang were just one chaotic event with infinite possibilities, then we'd never repeat a working universe.

Response: But this argument does not help you in the least. At the worst case, you are arguing that with one single chance in infinity we ended up with the just right universe, with the just right location for discovery out of infinite possibilities. This idea requires even more blind faith than infinite universes. You are saying it's statistically *impossible* to get it right, but it *just* happened and on precisely the first and only try. At least the infiniversalists have a slightly more tenable solution, they say there were infinite tries, and we are just one of those.

But the nail in the coffin for this is to remember that anything with an even slightly less than infinite chance of occurring would have occurred infinite times given infinite opportunities.[99] Given infinite tries, even chaos theory says all possibilities will eventually *repeat* themselves.

The only way to get any less than infinite universes requires a *non-*mechanistic agent. Unless you want to be irrational, there is simply no logical or rational way out of this.

Objection 18. I don't accept infinite universes and I don't accept the "designed for discovery" argument or the "fine tuning" argument. I think those were just parts of the initial conditions, thus naturally we ended up where we are. I don't think we need a "god" to manage each atom post Big Bang to get that.

Response: But this position makes no sense at all. First, at no time are we saying that Agent X *had* to manage anything post Big Bang.[100] The argument is that He could have simply fine-tuned the *initial* conditions and lit the fuse. Now don't think I'm a deist as you

---

[99] You might say: "each time would be a new try, i.e., even if you try flipping a coin 100 times, the chances of getting a heads on the 100th time is still just 50%." First, while that's true, the *aggregate* chance is not 50% because the chances of not getting a head at all in a sequence of tosses is far less than getting at least one or more tails in the sequence. Second, if you really believed that, why don't you apply that belief to abiogenesis? Each attempt at abiogenesis would be a brand new attempt and thus abiogenesis never occurs. You need the aggregate statistics for abiogenesis and parts of evolution (i.e., the initial successful mutations) to work. But the real answer is that if you throw a die with six faces 6000 times, you'd expect to get an even distribution of the faces. And if you found out that you seemed to get 2000 6's and no 5's you immediately suspect someone had monkeyed with the die.

[100] I think He does manage a few things, but if He has a free will He can "choose" to do so.

would be forgetting the "designed for discovery" points. Second, we are arguing that the statistical probabilities of the fine tuning and being located in an ideal place for the discovery of Agent X are so statistically minute that without infinite attempts you'd need utter superstitious blind faith to think it happened "magically" by sheer luck on the very first and only try. To clarify, to get the immensely fine-tuned universe that we have, there would have to be a very large number of universes, each of which was almost identical to the last and only different from the others in a minute way. And if you postulate even more than one "attempt" you are back to infinite universes or a non-mechanistic Agent X. In eternity, more than one equals infinite.[101]

Objection 19. You can't prove that God exists with 100% certainty, so I don't accept it.

Response: You are correct on the first part. But to be fair, I cannot prove anything 100%, nor can *you*. For example, philosophers have long noted that no one can prove that we didn't suddenly pop into existence 20 seconds ago with all our memories preprogrammed as well as our scars and the food in our stomachs preloaded. The question we must ask ourselves though is: Does this seem reasonable? At some point, we have to admit that it does not. But I don't see you going around saying that you give any credence to the "popped into existence 20 seconds ago" theory on the grounds that no one can prove it to be false with 100% certainty.

In the same way, we must look at what seems most reasonable. In this case, we have a choice between infinite universes and a non-mechanistic first cause.

Now of course you may think that having infinite alternate universes with Evil Spock or Evil "you" in many of them is true. But you can't prove it; are you seriously thinking that the average man on the street should blindly accept it? What other un-provable theory should we buy into? Why is this theory better than any other superstitious religion? When did blind unsubstantiated faith become the recommended belief system to be pushed by atheists?

---

[101] This crucial concept may the most difficult one in this book to grasp. Please reread Chapter Three if you are hazy on it.

Objection 20. No god exists; man believes in a god because he wants a god to exist.

Response: This assertion is illogical; it is a *non sequitur*. One cannot conclude the latter ("no god exists") just because of the former ("man wants to believe in a god"). I may want the sun to rise tomorrow, but my wanting the sun to rise or not wanting it to rise, has nothing to do with the reality of it rising. We are studying the reality of the necessity of a non-mechanistic extra dimensional personal first cause, not *my* desires for one.

Remember too, as we said at the beginning of this book. To refute this argument you have to show the facts are wrong or the logic is wrong. Not say, "Hey look Elvis."

And this argument works both ways: If you say God doesn't *exist* because I *want* Him to exist, I can turn that around and say God does not "*not exist*" because you *want* Him *not* to exist (because you are scared of being held morally responsible to a superior being). What logic is there in that? The fact of wanting or not wanting is not relevant to the facts and the logic that I have presented. If anything, wanting could be cited as evidence suggesting God put the wanting in us. I would not use that evidence as solid proof, but it provides an explanation that is just as viable an explanation as yours.

The only time wanting something to exist or not exist may be relevant is if you have absolutely no evidence to prove that something exists, like infinite universes, and yet insist that it does exist despite all the rational evidence that a non-mechanistic Agent X exists. In such a case the wanting relates to the psychology of believing, but that is totally outside of my argument and does not invalidate the argument.

Objection 21. What about the Quantum Universe Theory?

Response: The Quantum Universe Theory is in many ways a similar idea to the mechanistic agent creating infinite universes but with a few subtle differences. It says that there was an initial universe but now there are infinite universes in infinite dimensions and they are constantly multiplying. The basic idea is that any time a decision is made by anyone or anything, a new universe springs up for each possible action of that decision (note how this is different from having a mechanistic agent that randomly creates universes). Some atheists may incorrectly posit this as evidence that the first cause is a mechanistic agent constantly giving rise to universes. But here's the problem. The very first quantum universe (unless infinitely old) still needs a non-mechanistic first cause. Secondly, no one can ***prove*** the Quantum Universe Theory; science offers no evidence of it. It's an interesting theory with no evidence; perhaps it is great science fiction. But it's not verifiable. People are welcome to believe that if they want. But then they need to accept the fact that their basis of beliefs is also based on blind faith. And they must not accuse us of being the only ones with a faith, even though I would argue we have more evidence for our faith than they do for theirs. Ours is a rational faith based on evidence. Theirs is an irrational faith based on emotions.

Note that this answer also covers a gamut of issues that postulate un-provable theories of mechanistic agents. You can add mechanistic agents behind mechanistic agents behind other mechanistic agents but you end up at the same place. You need a non-mechanistic agent *or* you need infinite universes. Of the two alternatives to the God hypothesis, one is illogical (to postulate a mechanical agent) and the other is un-provable (that there are infinite universes) and rather fantastical. And if you are believing something with no rational evidence, that is called blind faith. If you are truly an atheist, blind faith would be a horrible thing to believe in, wouldn't it?

[*Repeated from a previous response*] this theory also has a lot of unbelievable side effects. Consider: if there are infinite universes, then by necessity there are universes where Earth exists but every alternative option has been taken. Every alternative and possible event has occurred. In one universe, in any given situation there has to be a world where if one person predicts the future it always comes to pass, or where the same person wins every lottery. Are you having as much trouble as I am with believing this?

I have one question about one of those universes, say Universe Y. Are there any atheists in that universe where the laws of probability don't seem to apply for certain scenarios? Anytime someone prays in that universe for an uncertain probabilistic thing, it comes to pass. In that universe, every time you buy a lottery ticket, and pray, you win. Any game you participate in, you win. I'd think there would be no atheists in that world because prayer always coincides with a favorable outcome in a game of chance (unless they are praying against each other, for instance, for a game).

Are you seriously proposing this? Actually now that I think about it, it would make a good Twilight Zone or Star Trek episode.

Objection 22. Just because there are infinite universes, why does there have to be one where we are on opposite sides of this issue? Those life forms could have evolved another way.

Response: Of course, assuming evolution is even possible, then they could have evolved another way, and there would be infinite ones that did. But there also would be ones that evolved identically to ours except in minor ways. Every possible combination of events must have taken place somewhere. Anything that is possible must have happened. In fact, if you think about it, there should also be multiple or actually infinite copies of our universe, where the other you and me are doing the exact same thing we are doing now. This is getting pretty farfetched for me to buy it. And that beat goes on: there are infinite me's out there doing exactly what I'm doing right now and infinite me's out there doing exactly what I'm doing but delayed by 1 second, or delayed by a billion years. When can I stop and laugh at the ridiculousness of this blind belief?

Objection 23. What about the Bud Theory?

Response: The Bud theory says we are a blip in a vastly larger universe. Or there are infinite smaller universes but they mechanistically reproduce by creating a small bud that breaks off from its parent universe every trillion years or so to form into another infinite universe.

Again, the problem here is we have no proof for these theories. And if you do subscribe to Occam's Razor as most atheists do, then you have to ask for the theory that requires the *fewest necessary* agents.[102] We don't need to argue if the theory with the fewest necessary agents is a non-mechanistic agent, or an infinite number of mechanistic ones, or infinite universes, or a small part of an even larger infinite universe, because it's obvious. The fewest necessary agents is a *single* Agent X.

Since the current evidence does not support the Bud theory, we may as well blindly believe that a great Serpent Spirit created the

---

[102] Occam's (or Ockham's) razor is a principle attributed to the 14th century logician and Franciscan friar, William of Occam. It basically says, "When you have two competing theories that make exactly the same predictions, the one that is has the fewest necessary agents or assumptions is the better." Note that it does *not* say, "The one which is least complicated, is the better" – because it's an issue of necessary agents, not of the complexity of those agents. Unless you can prove that a simpler agent works, you cannot apply the simplicity argument.

world as some cultures do. That blind belief would be equally as valid.

But the other problem with the Bud theory is that you end up with the accursed Infiniverse problem (discussed at great length in previous responses).

Objection 24. Why does our Agent X have to be a "spirit"? Why can't it be mechanistic matter from another universe? Or why can't it be a universe that caused another universe that caused another universe, etc.

Response: This is just another version of the Bud theory. You have a couple of variations here. Either each universe is a super universe in that it contains all the other universes, or each universe is an independent universe. But in all cases you have a non-mechanistic problem with infinite versions of you and me and that danged Poker game that makes it all ludicrous (*unless* there are no humans in any of the universes except for this one). But that means our Universe is unique and coincidently *also* designed for discovery (not to mention all the other arguments like the Moral argument, Resurrection argument, etc.) Quite a bit more improbability appears here, and one still can't prove any of it but must accept all on blind faith.

Objection 25. I don't accept the Big Bang Theory (yes, I've had atheists tell me this).

Response: If you are an atheist and don't accept the Big Bang Theory, your argument is not with me but with Lemaître, Hawking, Einstein, Hubble, Michealson, Morely, Friedmann, Gamow, Alpher and Herman and a host of others. As it is the current accepted theory in science, you would be arguing that you don't believe what is accepted by science and instead are going with your own gut feelings. I call that blind faith. It would be different if you had evidence showing the Big Bang theory was incorrect. Recall that atheists typically charge Christians and other with being irrational for disbelieving the "accepted" theory of neo-Darwinian evolution. I am not arguing that a theory's being "accepted" makes it true; I arguing that if you are going to reject an "accepted" theory, then you need evidence and reasoning to do so. Intelligent Design theorists, for example, offer evidence showing neo-Darwinian evolution is impossible and did not occur as the "accepted" theory describes it. Thus, if you refuse to accept the science of the Big Bang that is more validated than evolution (as it is predictive, unlike evolution), then surely you are taking an unsupported, dare I say superstitious, position.

Here's a further challenge to the atheist who rejects the Big Bang. You don't accept the Big Bang Theory, which is subject to scientific proof, measurable, in some ways testable, and most importantly able to predict things we can confirm. Yet, you accept neo-Darwinian evolution, which is not provable and has not been able to predict anything that couldn't be attributed to a different cause. You are condemning a strong theory and accepting a weak theory, it seems, because you don't like the consequences of the logic, not because of the merits of the theory. Why does the concept of a God scare you or bother you so much that you reject science for superstition?

Remember, too, that evolution does not necessarily disprove God's *existence*. It merely causes concerns about the inerrancy or translation of the first book of the Bible, and about the character of a God who creates species by a process of accidents, suffering and death. While I don't agree with them at all, some theists like Francis Collins and Dinesh D'Souza actually believe in Theistic Evolution. So you see, evolution is *not* an arrow through the heart of God. It does however cause serious theological problems with the concept of sin and salvation.

Objection 26. I accept the Big Bang but I don't accept the Singularity.

Response: Of course, if you say this you blindly believe things completely contrary to modern science. Are you sure you want to take this tack? Remember, not accepting something is not the same as refuting it. You have to show why the Singularity is not true. If you are arguing for the LQC theories, then see the previous objection about LQCs and also the link to William Lane Craig's response.

Furthermore, why do you think all those atheistic scientists out there like Calle are postulating infinite universes? It is precisely because they realize they are stuck with a finite universe (our Universe) and thus to avoid a God, they get stuck with mechanistic agents that lead to infinite universes.

But even if you don't accept the Singularity, you are still stuck. The Singularity is not the bane of your beliefs; it's the Big Bang and the non-eternal universe that's the thorn in your side. Even if you proved the Universe did not begin with a singularity but is part of an infinitely old collapsing and expanding universe, you are still stuck with the equivalent of an Infiniverse. Why? Because with infinite collapses and expansions you'd get infinite attempts at a universe, which means you get duplicates of every variation of reality (each with tiny differences) in the infinite recycling. So don't call it the Singularity, instead call it Fred, call it curved space, who cares, I certainly don't, it's a beginning event that either leads to infinite universes of some sort, or to a God.

Objection 27. I don't believe our Universe only began to exist at the Big Bang. Science is not convinced of this 100%. What if things existed before that?

Response: First, you are trying to refute Hawking and Einstein. They believed with evidence that everything in our Universe began to exist at the Big Bang. But second, even as you try to resolve your disagreement with them, you still have to deal with eternal mechanistic agents.

On the other hand, if you are arguing that other things exist *outside* our Universe, those things don't matter to the discussion unless one of those eternal things created our Universe. And if so, then it doesn't help you. Either those other things are mechanistic or they are non-mechanistic. If they are mechanistic, you need an eternal universe or infinite universes. If they are non-mechanistic, congratulations you've become a theist because the only other options, i.e., polytheism and deism, don't work. Polytheism is self-refuting (see the next objection) and deism was refuted within this book as we discovered it's reasonable to think the Earth was designed for discovery.

Objection 28. Why do you keep referring to other atheists' views? I don't care what other atheists think. This is not a religion and they are not our Popes.

Response: It's funny you should complain about that. I only quote atheists who have some authority in the field they are arguing for. That is, it's a valid appeal to authority. It's not like appealing to the Pope about science. It's appealing to a scientist about science. If I quote theistic scientists, then you would likely disregard them, saying, "Oh, of course they think that. They are theists." Thus I quote atheistic scientists. And you still complain! You can't have it both ways. I think the problem you are having is with the inevitable conclusion, the consequences of the logic, not with the actual data or logic.

Neil Mammen

Objection 29. Aliens did it (i.e., created the Universe).

Response: This theory does not fit the facts that we know about Agent X. To begin with, aliens would be at the most multi-dimensional and not *extra*-dimensional (outside the Universe). The Agent X we derived has to exist *outside* of time and space. If your aliens exist *within* the Universe then they do not predate the Universe and therefore do not qualify. If you are postulating extra-dimensional aliens with their own timeline, then you'd have to show me how they differ from God. Also, see the paper on our website www.NoBlindFaith.com under "writings" called "Can God create a stone so big that He cannot move it." That paper shows, using simple set theory, that only a ***single*** all-powerful being can exist, as *multiple* all-powerful beings or polytheism is self-refuting and self-contradictory.[103] So, at the end of your reasoning the result is only one extra-dimensional all-powerful "alien" that is no different from the Biblical definition of God. So if you really wish to call this God an alien, that's fine. He's certainly not terrestrial nor is He constrained by the 26 potential dimensions.

Objection 30. I don't accept the fact that everything that began to exist needs a cause.

Response: What? Seriously? Are you a 16th century superstitious peasant? I don't believe that you believe that. Okay sorry, I just had to say that.

Let's look at this carefully, as it was articulated to me in an email:

Of the staggeringly large number of things that exist, a vanishingly small number of them have been seen, or inferred, to have been caused. Observational bias leads humans to believe else wise.

I have no idea whether atoms are blinking in and out of existence all around us, though I'd guess it's not that common. Your statement might be correct, but you don't have - can never have - enough data points to prove it.

If we can't observe beyond the boundary of the start of the Universe, the best we may ever be able to do is speculate

---

[103] Note that the concept of the Trinity is that God is one being but three persons. Yes, I know you don't get that. But that's theology, not apologetics. It's important to realize that whoever came up with the idea of a Trinity that comprised of one being but three persons knew that you could not logically have more than a single supreme being (unlike all the Roman and Greek religions).

whether it popped into existence [here he's forced to try to claim there's a multiverse that caused everything; or illogically propose a mechanistic cause of a non-eternal event]. *A non-cause is far more reasonable than an intelligent cause; otherwise, you'll need to explain to me the cause for your first cause.*

First, it seems that this person has not really understood the argument, because he's trying to claim either the multiverse or a non-mechanistic non-eternal cause is what did it. This entire book logically refutes that very concept. My response to the above email would be: It seems that you are saying that you believe things randomly and supernaturally arise from nothing and have no cause (certainly not a natural cause), or that some initial universe that creates other universes supernaturally arose from nothing. You cannot prove these other universes exist, you can't calculate them, smell them, taste them, touch them, interact with them, see them, or use instruments to detect them. But you are firmly convinced that this invisible spaghetti monster exists and is the source of everything you *can* see touch, taste, smell, hear, and calculate.

Science today tells us that nothing comes from nothing. And yet this email unscientifically makes a superstitious claim that perhaps somewhere somehow some things come from nothing and just pop into existence (presumably because the scientific truth and logic leads to an inconvenient result).

Try this with a judge and jury. "Yes, your honor, my client is innocent. He was just minding his own business when the murder weapon suddenly popped into existence into his hands. After all, *of the staggeringly large number of things that exist, a vanishingly small number of them have been seen, or inferred, to have been caused. Observational bias leads humans to believe wrongly to the contrary.* The prosecutor's *statement might be correct, but* he doesn't *have - can never have - enough data points to prove it.* Surely we can't be so presumptuous to say that murder weapons never ever pop into people's hands."

Are you kidding me? Nobody should be buying this sort of irrational malarkey for a nanosecond.

I hope you forgive me for thinking this seems a bit like a superstitious ancient animistic belief more suitable to a peasant 1,000 years ago (not to make an ad hominem attack). Science is based on samples, observations, experimentation, and repeatability. Do you want to abandon all that and go back to the Dark Ages with witch burnings and the lot?

Most atheists before the 1950's would vehemently disagree with the email's point. In fact, they themselves declared the premise that only things that began to exist needed a cause, and if something like the Universe existed forever, it needed no cause. It was the basis for their insisting that the Universe had existed forever. It was their bedrock against religion.

It seems that the only reason a few atheists today try to posit that everything that begins to exist does *not* need a cause, (a concept that would be utterly laughed at a few years ago, you wouldn't get a science tenure with that sort of a statement), is because they *now* don't like the consequence of the logic. However, as long as they thought the Universe was eternal, *all* atheists embraced that very opposite conclusion. So forgive me if I think it's a bit weak to try to say that isn't true now that it hurts the atheist's case. It seems disingenuous and hypocritical. And if this is the atheists' strongest argument, I have to simply say, "Wow, their situation is direr than we imagined."

Second, if this is their premise, then the burden of proof is on the one making this unscientific baseless improvable claim.

For years, atheists charged theists with the burden of proof that an unseen entity exists because (they said) it's very unusual, there's no evidence for it, and it doesn't happen every day.

Now they turn around and try to say, "Ah, but perhaps things suddenly do pop into existence on their own, out of nothing."

It seems now the burden of proof to prove that things pop out of nothing is upon the atheist. Because it's very unusual, there's no evidence for it, and it doesn't happen every day, the burden of proof is on the person making the claim.

Honestly, I can't imagine you actually believe that and are only taking this ignorant peasant like point of view because you fear the logical consequences of what science tells us. *If that's your best argument, i.e., "things pop out of nothing," then atheism is the most superstitious of all beliefs.*

Consider how dangerous this line of argument is for an atheist. Once you argue that things could pop into being *uncaused* just because we've only studied a small number of all things, then you destroy your own basis to say that miracles can't happen, that people can't be healed, that people don't rise from the dead. After all, have you studied every single event in history? Once the atheist concedes that miracles can happen, then we can together look at the miracles documented in the Bible.

Let me address this one line specifically: *"A non-cause is far more reasonable than an intelligent cause, otherwise you'll need to explain to me the cause for your first cause."*

Remember, you can't turn around and punt this back at us saying: "What caused your God's existence?" Here's the key: the premise for science is that logically and rationally anything that *existed forever* needed no cause. Only things that began to exist needed a cause. Remember, if there were never a moment causally or temporally when something did not exist (which is the definition of "always existed"), it would not be able to have a cause. Back in the 1950's when atheists thought the Universe existed forever and needed no cause, they didn't go around asking, "What caused the Universe?" They logically realized that anything that exists forever needs no cause. In the same way, God existed forever and needs no cause.

Furthermore, the objection stated has nothing to stand on because you are not comparing apples to apples. Either you have an eternal mechanistic causer or you have an eternal *non*-mechanistic causer. But in *both* cases, you have an eternal *uncaused* causer. **Even atheists need an uncaused causer.** And in fact, there is no logical or rational room for a non-eternal uncaused causer, anywhere in science or philosophy. Provide me with counter evidence if you disagree.

I have to deal with one final completely amazing claim by the atheist email writer: *If we can't observe beyond the boundary of the start of the Universe, the best we may ever be able to do is speculate whether it popped into existence.*

What? We can only speculate whether it popped into existence? We can only speculate that we are here? What on Earth is this objector talking about? This is certainly not rational. Okay, maybe he means "it popped into existence uncaused," but as we've discussed this is the most unscientific concept ever. It's simply irrational and at that point why not abandon all science and logic and blindly believe whatever we wishfully desire. I really and truly just *don't* have enough faith to be an atheist.

Objection 31. But I don't buy the need for a first cause. I still think "nothing" created the Universe, it just popped into being. Maybe *inside* a universe nothing can pop into being, but if nothing exists outside it, then perhaps a universe can pop into being in *that* nothing.

Response: Sadly, many atheists adopt this fall back position. In so doing, they superstitiously reject science completely and hang on to something they cannot prove, blindly asserting that things can pop into existence. But here's the rub: "nothing" is also mechanistic. You can't have a single universe that pops into being from nothing. If one universe popped into being from nothing, then infinite universes must also have popped into being. And with that, we are back to the blind faith and that accursed Poker game. You can't see touch, taste, smell, hear, or measure these infinite universes, yet you blindly insist they exist. Surely, this is not more rational than believing in a non-mechanistic infinite being, especially in light of the other evidence.

Objection 32. Asserting that things that begin to exist must have a first cause is only a philosophical point, not a scientific point.

Response: This objection is just plain silly. A philosophical truth is transcendent unlike many scientific truths. Why? For two reasons: First, philosophical truths do not need a universe to be true (e.g. the laws of gravity do not exist outside the Universe and one can conceive of a universe with different laws of gravity. But there are no universes where 1+1 is not equal to 2 and you don't need a universe for that to be true). Second, philosophy is the father of science. Science cannot exist without the truths of philosophy. By the way, what do you think the Ph. stands for in Ph.D., a degree that even scientists get? It stands for Philosophy, as in Doctor of Philosophy.

In addition, when Pasteur first proved that life needs a cause and doesn't come from non-life and showed it with a scientific experiment, there were critics, but nobody really thought "Ah, well, that's not a scientific question, how dare Pasteur try to prove his theory using science and facts and logic." Why not then just come up with any sort of random theory and despite the overwhelming scientific evidence push it off as a philosophical issue? Sure, maybe things can come from nothing, but can you prove that? Or are you blindly hoping and believing that? When do I get to start using my brain again? But don't forget *even* if the Universe popped into being *without* a cause, you are still stuck with a mechanistic cause (because "nothing" is mechanistic) and thus those horribly unreasonable infinite you's and me's out there in infinite universes (and that doggone Poker game).

Objection 33. Quentin Smith, a well-known atheist, has claimed Hawking proposed a Wave Theory model of the Universe that shows the Universe is 95% probable without a first cause.
Response: Quentin Smith's proposal fails the most basic test of the Agent X analysis. In his proposal, he posits a timeless space, which is a 4-dimensional hyperspace near the beginning of the Universe. He says it is smaller than 10^{-35} meters in radius. He says that this hyperspace gave rise to the Universe and it has always existed.

But here's the problem. First, there is no evidence of this hyperspace and if time and space didn't exist at the Singularity, where did hyperspace magically come from? You can't solve a problem by making it more complex. Hyperspace is multidimensional space; it's *more* than just 4D space. Second and more damaging, even if we grant Smith his premise, this proposed "Smithian" hyperspace is a *mechanistic* agent. It has no free will and Smith has merely posited a mechanistic first cause that we have already dispensed with. He's merely pushed the problem back one more step. But that gains him absolutely nothing. And it violates the basic principles of physics.

Remember, if a mechanistic agent were going to give rise to the Universe, it would have done so in infinity past. This means the Universe would be eternally old. But it isn't eternally old.

As described repeatedly in this book, the other option is that the mechanistic agent would continue to give rise to infinite universes, and that idea fails on multiple fronts. Moreover, Smith's proposal also violates the fact that at the point of the Singularity there was no time, no space, and no other dimensions, because hyperspace is still space. It needs dimensions to exist. So that seems to violate the entire theory of the Big Bang and goes against science.

So Smith's basic premise fails the very simplest test, is un-scientific, and thus is not a rational explanation for the beginning of the Universe. Quentin Smith can make his mechanistic agent as small as he wants and as far back as he wants, but it's still a mechanistic agent with no free will and thus should have either given rise to the Universe an infinite time ago or have given rise to infinite universes. Since all evidences show the contrary of that, one can only surmise that Quentin Smith has irrational illogical faith in something un-provable and contrary to the evidences we have. I call that blind faith.

Notably, Smith only proposes this because he agrees that he needs a first cause that existed forever. Remember this for those of you who may propose that nothing can exist forever or we don't need a first cause. You can't have your cake and eat it too.

Objection 34. However small the chances are, there is the chance that...

Response: Chance is mechanistic. Any appeal to even infinitesimally small chance will get you in trouble with the infinite. Remember at the end of the day there are either infinite identical and infinite slightly different duplicates of you and me out there – or there is a God. Which seems more reasonable to you, my *unique* friend?

In addition, chance doesn't create anything. Chance is not a "thing" that can create. It's a probability. The probability of winning a $1M is not a $1M. Somebody had to create that $1M first.

Objection 35. But your defense is merely mocking the infinite universe idea.

Response: Not at all. I am just saying that it's not as reasonable as the non-mechanistic first cause option. All I'm doing is explaining the weirdness that you are forced to embrace when you blindly believe in infinite universes. And remember the same excuse you have about being unable to prove God applies to being unable to prove infinite universes. I could complain that it's hard to prove a negative. Although in this book and in the other books in the series, I am arguing that we can indeed prove God's existence is more reasonable than infinite universes.

Objection 36. The Time/Knowledge question: In a college debate with some students that I was assisting, one of the atheists asked this question, "How can you say that God existed before time? If there was no time, He could not have learned anything. Then how did He get the knowledge He needed to create the Universe and be God?"

Response: The raw truth is: this is a meaningless question. Of course, convincing an audience of this in a few seconds is another matter completely. But here's one way to provide the answer:

You are asking what happened before time began. You are asking me to philosophize about the possible explanations of "How

Agent X knows what He knows." But, in reality that is irrelevant. Agent X is timeless and immaterial, and has no need to learn.

Let me explain further:

1. The question is similar to a 2 dimensional being asking why a 3 dimensional being is not limited by 2 dimensions. The 2 dimensional being will have trouble understanding the exact nature of the 3 dimensional being and would have great difficulty imagining how the 3 dimensional being does something. To bring it back to the question: What you are asking in that question is "Why is Agent X which is outside of time not limited by time?" See the silliness here?

    Remember also that Agent X precedes the Universe causally but not temporally. For time did not exist at the point of the creation.

2. I never said that we know **all** the characteristics of Agent X. We derived only the **necessary** characteristics (i.e., free willed, non-mechanistic omnipresent, omnipotent, omniscient, personal); we did not derive **all** the characteristics and conditions. Nor did we say that I could explain where Agent came from because that is a meaningless question. In fact, my case rests on the fact that Agent X did not have to **come** from anywhere as we have repeatedly said. In the same way, why is it not possible for Agent X to not have to *learn* either? In addition, since Agent X is necessary for the Universe to exist, it is not unfathomable for science that Agent X always existed just as at one time it **was** not unscientific or unfathomable for science to derive that the Universe had always existed.

    What about transcendent truths, when did they start to exist? When did 1+1 become 2? Isn't it more rational to say 1+1 has always been equal to 2? It never *didn't* exist as a fact. Remember you need no physical universe for $1+1 = 2$.[104]

---

[104] I like to ask: When did 1+1 become equal to 2 and when did it know it? Now some may try to play games here. "What does 1 plus 1 mean?" they ask with a grin, "maybe it is 11. Maybe 1 means something different in another country like in Mexico where it's the name of a man (Juan)." But this is sheer childish disingenuousness. I gave you a mathematical equation, I used numerical tokens that are accepted to convey a precise concept; it's scientifically, logically, rationally, philosophically and historically precise. All mathematicians know exactly what I mean by this equation. If they don't, it's due to their ignorance and not because the equation is imprecise or lacking or unclear. So if you are unable to comprehend this mathematical equation, then say so and I will provide you with my child's first grade addition and subtraction primer for your education.

Neil Mammen

So I must ask: Are you trying to refute the premise that anything that always existed needs no cause or beginning? If so, you have a lot more people to convince than me, i.e., the bulk of the scientific community and lots of philosophers.

Furthermore, why don't you apply that rationale to the Universe? You see, until we discovered that the Universe had a beginning, we also accepted the notion that the Universe had no beginning, yet at that time, we didn't see any arguments from your side that the Universe had to grow to exist nor did we see your side arguing, "Well, where did the Universe come from?" It's a little dubious for a single individual to contradict the standard scientific thought, changing the requirements just now. You may choose to do so, but please do not assume that you are doing so logically or scientifically unless you can prove what you say. Until that point, what you say is purely an opinion and not a rebuttal.

3. Your argument indicates a linear form of thinking (like Khan[105]). Remember if there is no time, you cannot impose a linear sequence of events on things like knowledge or being. Nor can you impose it on non-linear beings. The non-mechanistic first cause that is required to bring about the Singularity is a non-linear entity not constrained by time, space, or any dimensional constraints at all.

    Moreover, if you give credence to the Infiniverse or collapsing and expanding universes (needed to support the idea that there is no free-willed first cause), then what happens in between the collapsing and expanding? If time stops in between, how did the next expansion start? Or if one universe gives rise to another and physics says at the start of each universe there was no time, then how did the next universe start if time stopped? Did it only stop in the new spawned universe? The illogic twists into knots. Of course, if you say that one spawned another, then you are back to the infinite universe theory and your objection is meaningless because even if we answered it, you'd just jump back and cling to the blind faith that led you to an Infiniverse.

4. At the point of the Singularity, there was no time and there was no space. Yet the Big Bang occurred. Using your argument, the Big Bang could never occur because time did not exist yet.

---

[105] As in "Wrath of" ... Okay, the *Star Trek* movie reference was too tempting.

However, we know the Big Bang occurred and we know that "causally prior" to time coming into existence there was no time. Thus, there are things here that you cannot conceive of but science tells us can occur causally despite there being no time. Agent X/God does *not* become impotent when He is outside of time, not any more than the Singularity was impotent to cause or develop into the Big Bang before time existed. In addition, using that argument you are then again trying to argue that the Singularity had no cause and we know that science tells us that anything that begins to exist needs a cause. The Singularity began to exist, so it needs a cause. Of course, you could try to argue that the Singularity **is** Agent X, but we've already proven it can't be because it's mechanistic.

5. Back to Agent X and learning: As we said, Agent X has always existed, thus He does not need to learn. Just because you as a human need to learn, that does not mean Agent X needs to learn. You will die one day. Agent X cannot die because He is outside of time and eternal by necessity (remember we've proven that at some point something eternal had to exist that was non-mechanistic). There are a myriad of differences between you and Agent X. Thus, there is no logical or rational reason to impose your limitations and requirements on Agent X. You already know that Agent X is extra-dimensional and you and realize we are not. So what makes you think your other limitations (that are not transcendent) must be limitations for Agent X? Returning to our example, think about this logically: by necessity Agent X's knowledge is as transcendent as $1+1 = 2$. Everything that Agent X knows, He's known from all eternity. There was never a point when He was not transcendent or omniscient. Absolute knowledge is part of the very nature of an infinite being and He could no more cease to be God or ever have not been God than He could ever cease to know all or ever not have known all. It seems your thinking is trapped in a very close-minded illogical little box.

Objection 37. A first cause that is uncaused makes no sense outside of the Universe, for if the first cause is outside of time, and time begins at the Singularity then how did it cause the Universe to exist?

Response: This is actually a subset of the objection we just responded to, i.e., "You need time for something to occur, but at the point of the Singularity there was no time." It seems a point that many of my atheist friends get stuck on. Here's the problem with this objection. This objection has nothing to do with an intelligent agent. Chances are you are only making this objection because of the implications of the intelligent agent. Even if nothing caused the Big Bang, you are still stuck, how did "nothing" cause the Universe to exist if time began at the Singularity. See the problem? The universe began to exist at the same time as time. So how did it begin to exist if there was no time? You can't solve the time dilemma by getting rid of the cause. Yet here we are; we exist. Time began to exist, so how did time begin to exist before there was time? This objection has absolutely nothing to do with whom or what created the Universe. It's a red herring.

There are many possible solutions. They range from alternate time dimensions to causality without temporality (illustrated by the example of a ball sitting on a cushion for all eternity – there is no temporal relationship but there is a causal relationship).[106]

This is not a problem you have with *us* theists. This is a fundamental problem you have with *all* Big Bangists, even the atheist variety. Are you sure you want to argue with them? Your only solution is to reject the Big Bang or reject that fact that time started at the Big Bang. Neither of those positions find much support in facts or reason.

Notice too, having an alternative time dimension that is outside of our Universe hurts the atheist case because it brings back in full force the problem of needing a non-mechanistic free will agent. So don't go there, it just doesn't help you.

Objection 38. How can you argue about what happened before the Singularity? Nobody knows what happened before it, it's meaningless to argue it. Or: How do you know that all the laws of physics and causality don't break down before the Singularity?

Response: If you'll forgive me, this seems to be simply a copout. We cannot say that we just do *not* know what happened before the

---

[106] As I said in an earlier footnote, that example uses matter and that needs time to exist. So a better example is 1+1 = 2. Here's a causality that is not temporal. In other words, since 1+1 was always equal to 2, and the addition is the cause of the 2, but the addition did not occur in time or space, so we have here an eternal causality without any temporality.

Singularity and thus beg off the discussion. True, the laws of physics do not apply because they are materially/dimensionally constrained. However, logic and rationality still apply, they are not limited to time or space. You would have a tough time on your hand to argue that prior to the Singularity, logic and rationality cease to exist (i.e., you can't say 1+1 was not equal to 2). Why? Because it hurts the atheist's case. If logic ceases to exist before the Singularity, then you cannot argue *logically* **about** logic ceasing. It makes no sense to use logic to claim logic itself was not valid before the Singularity.[107]

As we *are* logically trying to explain what happened before the Singularity, we can logically argue everything we have logically presented so far about the cause of the Singularity is indeed logical (hmm…sounds a little repetitious). Do my atheist friends really want to propose an illogical and thus feelings-based or blind faith solution to events before the Singularity? I thought that was the accusation against us theists. Have the tables turned?

But my atheist friends may insist: "That's the point!" At this point logic ceases to exist, so we cannot argue anything about it. Consider, however: any claim that logic did not exist before the Universe existed is self-refuting. The very statement that something does not exist means you are claiming that existence is different from non-existence. But that's a claim about logic – it's also a claim about the law of non-contradiction. What's more, it's also a validation of the law of addition (i.e., before something existed we have nothing, a zero). We add one universe or one law of logic and you have 0+1 = 1. Do you see how silly it is to claim that there was a time when logic or mathematics did not exist? The very statement presumes it always existed. You can't escape from it.

Yet even if we ignore the objection's logic problems, the atheist faces another quandary. He must now admit that despite the very logical argument that we have presented, he has abandoned that argument for one that has no logic. Again, I'm not sure about you, but given two theories, one that appeals to illogic and one that appeals to logic and fits the observable data, I'd stick with the latter.

---

[107] This is a self-refuting statement also known as a Suicide Statement. (See the writings on Suicide Statements at www.NoBlindFaith.com for some fun with other suicide statements like, "There is no absolute truth!" or "It's wrong to force your morality on others." Both are ridiculously illogical and/or hypocritical statements – can you detect why?)

As Mr. Spock of *Star Trek* fame would have said, "It is ...after all... logical." We contend simply that *our* derivation is **more** scientific, **more** logical, and **more** reasonable than **yours**.

Objection 39. But if God is outside of Nature, then God cannot be logical or rational; logic and rationality came into being at the Singularity.

Response: We have previously explained how this contention is false. You can't logically argue about something's origins if you say that logic ceases to exist at some point within the relevant time frame.

The more rational thought is that logic and rationality have always existed and are not part of the natural or supernatural universe. It's extra-natural. It exists apart from space, time and energy. It exists apart from any universe.

For instance, 1+1 did not come into existence as part of the natural or physical universe. In fact, it did not come into creation at the Big Bang and is not dependent even on the other 6 and perhaps 22 unseen dimensions. You don't need matter or time for 1+1 = 2. There are no feasible universes where 1+1 = 3. Thus, 1+1 is a transcendent truth. And if you believe in the Infiniverse (as your excuse to avoid believing in a free-willed Agent X), then are you suggesting that there are zones in between those universes where 1+1 is not = 2? This is irrational, whoops there's that word again.

And do you really want to argue that your defense against my *rational* argument about God is to be *irrational*? It seems the tables have been turned.

In fact, while I won't spend time on it here, we could easily show that rationality *has* to be a characteristic of the first cause. Just as we proved omniscience and omnipresence, a logical argument can be used to derive a number of other characteristics of the first cause (not all, but a fair number), e.g., rationality, logic, mathematical principles, moral principles etc. All of these are inherent and necessary characteristics of the first cause. They are part of the necessary nature of God. They are all transcendent and exist independent of all physical or temporal things.

Objection 40. Philosophy is dead or I don't believe in Philosophy.

Response: That's a philosophical statement. So if it's dead or you don't believe in it, you've just refuted yourself. Philosophy is the father of science; logic and rational thinking are based on philosophy. Underlying science is the philosophy that *if* things are consistent, repeatable and make sense, *then* we can create a scientific principle out of it. The philosophy of science includes the idea that you should prove things by experimentation. Even the scientific method is a philosophical statement. Why? *Because the scientific method is not **scientifically** provable.* So, if you abandon philosophy, then you abandon science and you become akin to a superstitious peasant following illogical myths that you've invented.

Objection 41. But new Quantum Physics disproves the Singularity; or you are behind the times, the Big Bang theory you posit is old news. Now they don't think there *ever* was a Singularity, things have changed.

Response: These claims are false. To provide the best response without taking up too much space here, I'll refer you to Dr. William Lane Craig who provides an excellent response on his web page. The responses are a bit technical but complete www.NoBlindFaith.com/CraigQ48.htm[108]

Objection 42. But most people don't define God as an extra-dimensional, free-willed, non-mechanistic being.

Response: Really? Just because people don't use those words, it doesn't mean that's not their definition. Look: I have a horizontal transportation device that has an internal combustion engine mounted on a vehicle resting on vulcanized rubber pneumatic wheels that use friction along a plane to give it vectored acceleration in the x-axis. Translate that to English: we have an automobile. Sure, that long winded description is not what most people call it, but that's one possible technical description of it. If I were to work backwards or forwards, I'd still end up with the same thing. So it's irrelevant that they don't use the technical words. Do most Christians believe that God is omnipresent? Yes; extra dimensionality seems to allow that. Do they think He has free will? Yes; then He's non-mechanistic. Do they think He has a mind? Yes; then He is not a mechanistic machine or a photon. Do they think He wants humans to engage in a relationship with Him? Then He's personal. I'm not sure what the complaint is here. That's how they envision Him to be, the technical terms matter little. They are still accurate descriptions.

---

[108] Or www.reasonablefaith.org/site/News2?page=NewsArticle&id=6115

Ultimately, even if *nobody* thought of God that way, that means nothing. As an atheist and part of an ever-decreasing minority,[109] you surely don't believe that what the majority believes is automatically true? We've determined the character of Agent X. The atheist says this agent does *not* exist despite all the current scientific, rational and logical proof. So what will you do about that proof? Abandon it for a superstitious Infiniverse theory that can't be proven?

Objection 43. Our space-time started with the Big Bang but that doesn't mean other universes' time didn't exist before us or doesn't exist at the same time as us.

Response: The fundamental problem remains: no one can prove these other universes exist. It's un-falsifiable and thus unscientific. But in contrast, we *know* certain things scientifically about *our* Universe and rationally about the cause of our Universe (as shown in this book). Any postulation about some *other* universe is purely blind faith because we cannot reason it out nor can we prove it. It doesn't mean it's wrong, it just means it's unscientific since science can't prove or falsify it. So we can *only* postulate it as a possibility and then we have to admit that there's no way to prove it. There's no rational basis for this Infiniverse idea. The Infiniverse could be a pink unicorn and you would not be able to prove it or disprove it. Furthermore, you can't prove that any dimensions existed before the Big Bang. All indications are that nothing existed before.

Here's the other problem. You'd also have to prove that any dimension of time that is outside of the Universe had to be part of another yet *infinite* universe. Let me explain.

If our Universe is part of some sort of co-joined multiverse, but that multiverse had a *common* time factor that it shared with all multiverses as this objection postulated, then that multiverse would itself have to be infinitely old or composed of additional multiple universes without a common time dimension. Why? Because if not, then *that* multiverse would need a non-

[109] The number of atheists has shrunk in the population every year since 1970. In comparison, Christianity has grown at a rate of 60,000 Christians every single day. If you use the number of 2B as the number of Christians in the world, you come up with a growth rate of 2.33% but in reality, most of this growth is through conversions not births. When you realize that only 0.5B Christians are actually doing the witnessing, Christianity may actually be growing at an amazing clip of around 8% or more a year. It's set to double every 7 years.

mechanistic first cause. The only way this would work is if we are part of a multiverse with infinite other unrelated universes (the Infiniverse). Does that make sense? It's a strong restriction, but it exists logically. The upshot is: we've created a made-to-order universe that we can't prove exists. Why not create the flying spaghetti monster of Dawkins?

So frankly, I hope you understand my not buying it. It's just a lot of blind faith that you have in a postulate that cannot be proven. Surely you understand how any *thinking* person would be skeptical of a theory that has *no* evidence for it whatsoever and gets subsequently more complicated the more you look into it. It's a nice theory. But it's as valid as the multi-unicorn or the multi-flying-spaghetti-monster theory. However, in contrast, the concept of an extra-dimensional free-willed first cause is quite rational and quite logical and fits within everything we know about intelligence and the Universe that we *can* measure. In fact, the intelligent Agent X theory *fits* with everything we *do* know about our Universe. Now I'd admit that if that were the *only* thing we had to prove an intelligent Agent then perhaps one could argue that your multiverse spaghetti monster was as plausible as my free-willed personal Agent X. But as I said, that's only one of at least 6 categories of evidence. When taken together the weight of rationality and plausibility is on the side of a free-willed Agent X.

Objection 44. In physics, M-theory is a proposal that unifies the five ten-dimensional superstring theories as limits of a single 11-dimensional theory. Though a full description of the theory is not yet known, the low-energy dynamics are known to be super gravity interacting with 2- and 5-dimensional membranes...

Response: I don't mean this as a put down but I find it interesting when people grasp at a theory they don't understand to bail them out of a theory they *do* understand but hate the consequences of. It's one thing to be able to conclusively prove a scientific theory but surely, you see my skepticism when you say you don't understand M-theory but you expect it will solve the problem of needing a free-willed non-mechanistic agent.

It actually doesn't and it's like the "God of the Gaps" accusation leveled against theists. Supposedly, we theists can't understand something so we say "God did it." But in this case, you can't solve something and you say: "The Infiniverse did it." But the difference is crucial. We theists *derived* the seven characteristics of

Agent X logically. We didn't force fit the data. We got there rationally with evidence and showing it seems more reasonable than having infinite universes (where one universe out there where you and I are having this same argument but *you* are the one who wrote this book).

As for M-Theory, it really does *not* help your situation. It merely postulates another dimension to tie the 10 known ones together. M-Theory does not alleviate the need for a non-mechanistic first cause. "Branes" are mechanistic and worse, they did not exist in the Singularity or before it, as far as science tells us (see some of the previous objections). So how can they *cause* the Singularity?

Objection 45. The Heisenberg Uncertainty Principle (HUP) says things can pop out of nothing.

Have you actually studied the HUP? You cannot retreat to the Heisenberg Uncertainty principle, because it does not help you. All Heisenberg proved was that you cannot tell *both* the position and the momentum of a particle with any particular arbitrary precision. It does **not** say "things pop into existence without a cause." What it says is that in quantum mechanics, there are no states that describe a particle with both a definite position and a definite momentum. The more precise the position calculation, the less precise the momentum calculation. That's it. No magical particles or universes ceasing to exist or popping into existence. Just a limitation as to the accuracy of two specific measurements at any given time.[110] It also says nothing about us not being able to know if the particle exists at all. After we know it exists; we just can't measure two of its characteristics with any simultaneous precision. Sorry – no universes are popping out of this theory either. And remember even if that weren't the case, it would be mechanistic.

Objection 46. You are proposing the supernatural as a solution. That's not scientific.

Response: I love this objection. I wish I had been asked this before Casey Luskin, Cornelius Hunter, Ray Dennehy and I had debated evolutionist Eugenie Scott and ACLU Lawyer Eric Rothschild at the Commonwealth Club (broadcast on National Public Radio), because then I would have thought about it earlier and would have been able to give them a different answer. Here's what my answer would be

---

[110] One of my degrees is in Solid State Physics. www.aip.org/history/heisenberg/p08.htm

today.

1. You claim that the Universe came from nothing. You certainly can't call that natural. Is it scientific to assume that things come from nothing all the time? Suppose I walk up to you and say, "I created this clump of clay from nothing." Would you believe me or think I'd lost my marbles? Would you think I was a scientist?

   So any time you postulate that the Universe came from nothing, you are immediately postulating an unnatural unusual event. And when you say it happened, you are forced to claim that it happened outside our four dimensions because those dimensions came into being *after* the Big Bang. So we know that it must be a supernatural event.

2. You say that life came from no life. You certainly can't call that natural either. Is it scientific to assume that the law of abiogenesis is being violated on a daily basis? If I walk up to you and say, "I created a living creature from this clump of clay," would believe me, or again think I've lost my marbles? So when you say life came from non-life, thereby contradicting a known scientific law, you are postulating another unnatural unusual event.[111]

   So what can we conclude? At least 2 unnatural, unusual events have happened in the history of the world and at least one of them was a supernatural event. Well, if 2 can happen, why not 3? Why not 5? The atheist has no ground to object at this point – none. This works both ways. If the atheist can plead a supernatural cause to the Universe and claim it is scientific, then theist can too. Why does the introduction of intelligence and free will suddenly cause something supernatural and unusual to be unscientific when *we* use it, but not when *you* use it?

   Yet here's what atheists themselves say, showing a rather non-scientific and non-rational streak:

   > ...*we have a prior commitment, a commitment to materialism. It is not that the methods and institutions of science somehow compel us to accept a material explanation of the phenomenal*

---

[111] Note too, abiogenesis could not have just happened once. For life to persist, it would have to have happened billions of times, until one of those "living cells" survived long enough to multiply. See Lee M. Spetner, *Not by Chance!: Shattering the Modern Theory of Evolution*, (Brooklyn, NY: Judaica Press, 1998), 54-57 (This describes how the population genetics statistics show that a mutated organism with a positive survival value will be likely wiped out by random environmental events before ever reproducing and transmitting the favorable mutation).

world, but, on the contrary, that we are forced by our a priori adherence to material causes to create an apparatus of investigation and a set of concepts that produce material [author's note: think "limited to 4D"] explanations, no matter how counter-intuitive, no matter how mystifying to the uninitiated. Moreover, that materialism is absolute, for we cannot allow a Divine Foot in the door.[112]

They were refusing to allow any multidimensionality (i.e., non-materialism) into the equation, yet science itself says by necessity there are things far beyond the material 4 dimensions. There *are* things outside the dimensions.

Let's go a step further, because we can't stop at just the Big Bang and abiogenesis. Consider the evolution argument. If evolutionists plead billions of highly improbable events of speciation by beneficial mutation, then why can't theists propose improbable events as well? For example, the resurrection of a dead person to life, caused by an intelligent agent?

So if the Big Bang and abiogenesis and evolution are accepted as scientific, what audacity must you have to then say that *any* supernatural, unnatural, or unusual event is not scientific? That I think is the real question and the burden of proof is upon you to explain the apparent self-contradiction.

Furthermore, I have shown that it is indeed scientifically and logically reasonable to believe that multidimensional space exists. And in this multidimensional space, multidimensional objects could exist which could intersect our 3D space. Now if objects can exist, it is rational to say that creatures may also exist.

Therefore, not only do we have an equal rational basis for an extra-dimensional being but we also have an equal rational basis for multidimensional beings. So we know multiple dimensions exist. Why does it suddenly become unscientific to propose that multidimensional or extra-dimensional *intelligent* beings can exist when all the rational and logical evidence points to that possibility? The only issue here is one of intelligence. Once a multidimensional or extra dimensional intelligent being is shown to be possible, then the argument shifts to consider whether it is probable or not.

---

[112] Lewontin, Richard. "Billions and Billions of Demons." *New York Review of Books*, Jan 4, 1997.

Objection 47. How can you say that God needs no cause? Despite your previous explanations, I refuse to agree that: anything that has existed forever needs no cause, or that everything that begins to exist needs a cause.

Response: This objection requires a repeat of arguments set forth in this book. Let me boil them down here. Consider first: "Anything that has existed forever needs no cause."

If something never began to exist, then nothing could *causally* precede it. For something to be the cause of something else, it would have to precede it causally. But if that thing existed forever, it could never be preceded.

You may claim you believe that this is false, but for centuries scientists never had a logical or rational problem with something that always existed needing no cause. To refute this long-settled concept, you need to present some philosophical or scientific information that would change this logic. Perhaps you wish to come up with a new definition for the phrase "existed forever." You wish it to now mean, "It didn't really exist forever because there was some point at it which was not there and had to be 'made'."

Perhaps the truth is that you are saying, now that you know the Universe is not eternal, you don't *like* the fact that anything *else* besides the Universe could exist without a cause. It was no surprise when atheists in an earlier time said this:

> *Philosophically, the notion of a beginning of the present order of Nature is repugnant to me ... I should like to find a genuine loophole.*

Arthur Eddington[113]

These atheists realized the Big Bang's "beginning of the Universe" would cause major problems for their position; they had been comfortably relying upon the Universe existing forever and needing no cause. Your denying a fundamental idea of science and philosophy puts you in an indefensible position even with the prior crop of atheists. This should make you suspicious about any of your own claims about really wanting to know the truth. Could it be that you've put yourself in a box and you'll only accept that which you **want** to be true, not that which is actually more reasonably true?

---

[113] Arthur S. Eddington, "The End of the World: from the Standpoint of Mathematical Physics," *Nature*, 127 (1931): 447-53, 450, doi:10.1038/127447a0 (accessed November 25, 2012).

Neil Mammen

You might assert: "Those older atheists *were* stupid and ignorant to think that if the Universe existed forever it would need no cause. I'm a more enlightened atheist."[114]

Yet without new scientific or philosophical data, your stance is really unsupportable. It would seem that you are operating on feelings or blind faith at this point. Note those old atheists only found one new piece of relevant info, i.e., that the Universe had a beginning. That one item did not amount to a valid reason to abandon the concept that something could exist forever. Knowing the Universe has a beginning does not logically prove that anything that existed forever needs no cause.

Maybe you will say, "Now that we know the Universe didn't exist forever, we know that there's "no thing" that can exist forever. So you must show me something that exists forever for me to accept that such a thing could exist."

Okay, I will: Transcendent Truths. For instance $1+1 = 2$. Here is something that is eternal. It exists forever. It needs no universe to be true. It was true before any universe existed and will be true after. There are no feasible universes where $1+1$ is not equal to 2. Even when the Universe has died a heat death, $1+1$ will still be equal to 2 and for all eternity after that. There was never a time when $1+1$ was not equal to 2 and there never will be. Similarly, deductive logic and reasoning supply Transcendent Truths.

Let's look at the further consequences of claiming that "no thing" can exist forever.

It still means you have a problem with most other current, post Big Bang atheists. If "no thing" can exist forever, what gave rise to the Universe? Even atheists who were around after the Big Bang discovery have posited that hyperspace or some eternal *agent* caused the Big Bang. Quentin Smith suggested this, obviously not realizing that the Big Bang indicates that there were no dimensions prior to the Singularity and hyperspace is multidimensional which means it needs dimensions. But even Quentin postulates that this hyperspace

---

[114] Of course, you would also have to then admit that if sometime in the future we found out that the Universe had in fact existed forever and everyone was wrong, you'd start looking for a cause for it. Why don't I buy that for a minute? It's seems to me that the difference here is that you are afraid of a God existing, or you blindly hate the idea of having to be responsible to someone. Let me assure you it's not a very large burden. In fact it's a very freeing burden. Partly because all those laws that you hate are actually given for your protection. Not for your condemnation. See www.J3IP.com for a book about this.

could have existed forever. He, for one, apparently has no problem even with things existing forever. I'm not saying that you must accept Smith's reasoning. But I must ask what good reason do you have to not accept that? How do you refute him?

Am I appealing to atheistic authority too much? Okay, let's think logically about this. What is the basis for thinking that nothing can exist forever? If time does not exist, then even the word "forever" must mean something different from what you are thinking it means. If time began to exist at some point, then something must have existed causally before it to cause it, (note I said cause-ally before it, not temporally before it). Simple deduction says that whatever existed causally before the Singularity must exist outside of time and space. Or to put it more simply: whatever caused time and space to exist, must not itself be constrained by time and space.

You might speculate: "Maybe the Universe popped out of nowhere."

But that does not supply a scientific or philosophically acceptable premise (and we deal with this superstitious belief in this Objection Appendix in great detail). Note again something existing forever *is* a scientific and philosophically acceptable premise. At least it *was* considered scientific by every scientist as late as 80 years ago and atheists since then have not found any new information about existence in that time to refute it. No, quantum theory does *not* allow something to come from nothing (go back and read your physics textbooks. Quantum fluctuations are not a magic genie and - don't forget they are mechanistic). So why do you wish to propose an unscientific "popped from nowhere" premise?

Wait, there's more. Remember, again, anyone who postulates that infinite universes exist must admit that anything that exists forever needs no cause. Why do I say that? It's simple: because that's the criterion for not needing a cause. That is why some argue that since there are infinite universes, we don't need a cause. It's a tacit admission that any time you have something or some things that existed forever you don't need a cause for them. This is a rather self-defeating approach you are taking. The minute you propose that things pop into existence, you are saying all those other atheists who depend on infinite universes existing to avoid the personal first cause are just plain wrong or stupid.

Scientifically we know that every time we see something begin to happen, we know (or we certainly presume) it must have a cause. You can repeat this experiment endlessly in triple blind tests and you'll come to the same scientific conclusion. Nothing can come from nothing. Everything that begins to exist must have a cause.

On a lay person's daily living level, suppose you were walking around one day and you hear a bang and ask: "What caused that bang?" I say, "Nothing." You'd say, "Don't be stupid man! Bangs don't just happen for no reason."

If you are right about those little bangs, then so much more so about Big Bangs! Is there something scientific in the nature of the size of the bang that makes it not need a cause? There isn't. As for an uncaused bang, that's not scientific, it's not common experience even, it's fantasy. Thus the tables are turned. You ought not to keep insisting on an irrational solution as an alternative to a rational and logical solution that I've proposed?

But what if nothing caused the Big Bang. We may as well look at that point again (in case you've not read all the previous objections); remember it turns out that that doesn't solve your problem. Because, if nothing caused the Big Bang you are back in trouble with the mechanistic agent. If nothing caused the Big Bang, then either the Universe should be infinitely old or there should be infinite number of them. One is not true and the other can only be believed with blind faith. Though this sounds confusing, "nothing" is also mechanistic. It doesn't help you to appeal to nothing as the cause of the Big Bang.

So here's the rub:

1. There is no scientific evidence that can show any thing that begins to exist needs *no* cause. There is also no philosophic or logical premise to hold this belief. Therefore, we can conclude it is unscientific and superstitious to blindly believe something directly contrary to everything we have measured, observed, calculated, or reasoned.

2. There is no philosophic or logical refutation for something eternally existing. Until about 40 years ago, atheistic scientists seemed not to have a problem with the concept. I have never seen somebody seriously argue that it is impossible for something to exist forever (Feel free to provide an argument if you have one.) Many things exist eternally uncaused. For example, deductive logic exists eternally, and $1+1 = 2$ has always been true eternally. It never began to be true. The fact $1+1 = 2$ never began to be true and it has no cause. (Because that arithmetic fact is mechanistic, God did not have to cause it either.)

So, we are left with the original premises accepted by a

majority of scientists, be they atheists or theists: **anything that existed forever needs no cause, and anything that begins to exist needs a cause.**

To just assert these premises are wrong is easy – anyone can assert anything. I'm challenging you to prove them wrong against all the logic and scientific evidence presented in this book.

Let me repeat what we said earlier about eternal agents needing no cause. It's quite simple and logical. If anything existed forever, then there's no point in time or space or causality when it did not exist. So nothing can causally precede an eternal agent. If nothing can precede it causally, then it can have no cause.

The Kalam Cosmological Argument: Though I do not depend on every part of it, nor am I arguing for each formal part of it in this book, I've added William Lane Craig's formulation of the ancient Kalam Cosmological Argument as it will provide you with a more comprehensive argument:

1. Whatever begins to exist has a cause of its existence.
　　This is simple science and logic.
2. The Universe began to exist. [Proven in the 1950's to not be infinitely old, i.e., refuting collapsing/expanding theories]
　　2.1 Argument based on the impossibility of an actual infinite:
　　　　2.11 An actual infinite cannot exist.
　　　　2.12 An infinite temporal regress of events is an actual infinite.
　　　　2.13 Therefore, an infinite temporal regress of events cannot exist.
　　2.2 Argument based on the impossibility of the formation of an actual infinite by successive addition:
　　　　2.21 A collection formed by successive addition cannot be actually infinite.
　　　　2.22 The temporal series of past events is a collection formed by successive addition.
　　　　2.23 Therefore, the temporal series of past events cannot be actually infinite.
　　2.3 Confirmation based on the expansion of the Universe.
　　2.4 Confirmation based on the thermodynamic properties of the Universe.
3. Therefore, the Universe has a cause of its existence.
4. If the Universe has a cause of its existence, then an uncaused, personal Creator of the Universe exists, sans creation
　　4.1 Argument that the cause of the Universe is a personal Creator:
　　　　4.11 The Universe was brought into being either by a

mechanically operating set of necessary and sufficient conditions or by a personal, free agent (i.e., non-mechanistic).

4.12 The Universe could not have been brought into being by a mechanically operating set of necessary and sufficient conditions.

4.13 Therefore, the Universe was brought into being by a personal, free agent.

4.21 The Creator is uncaused.

4.211 An infinite temporal regress of causes cannot exist. (*See* 2.13, 2.23 above)

5. Therefore, an uncaused, personal Creator of the Universe exists, sans creation.

For more information and a defense of the Kalam Argument, please see Dr. Craig's website: www.WilliamLaneCraig.com.

I recommend that you also download his debates with atheists and buy all his books and CDs. It will be well worth your time especially if you are an atheist. If you are wrong, it would be worth your "time" to find out.

Objection 48. Quantum Mechanics indicates that things occur without a cause. For instance if there are two particles of uranium that are identical, one will decay without any cause, while the other wont. So things happen without a cause all the time.

Response: This objection confuses a lot of things. First a uranium particle is not "nothing" so you can't really compare the cause of the creation of the Universe from nothing to the cause of a thing that preexists acting a certain way for an unknown reason. You are confusing a "reason" for an action by an existing object with the reason for something popping into existence out of nothing. These are not the same use of the word "cause". The particle already exists, so the "cause" of the particle decaying *is* the particle. The Universe does not already exist so the cause of the Universe *cannot* be itself.

Second, there over 10 different theories about why a particle of uranium decays, only 1 of them posits no cause. And even if we chose that theory, this is science of the gaps. All you can say is that *you* don't know *yet* why the first particle decayed vs. the second. You can't say there is no good reason.

Objection 49. Fine Tuning - there are two possible objections:
  a. **Fine tuning has been refuted.**
  b. **The fine tuning is all anthropomorphic and life could have developed differently if the numbers were different.**

Response to a: To begin with, if you think fine tuning has been refuted, your argument is not with me but with luminaries like Dr. Dennis Scania, the distinguished head of Cambridge University Observatories, Dr. David D. Deutsch, Institute of Mathematics, Oxford University, Dr. Paul Davies, author and professor of theoretical physics at Adelaide University, Sir Fred Hoyle and many others like them. Yes, this *is indeed* an appeal to authority but this is precisely their field of expertise and they can speak about it authoritatively. So, you'd have to refute them first.

A simple web search for "fine tuning of the Universe quotes" will yield many quotes from these and other astrophysicists.

Response to b: Of the fine tuning evidence I've provided, only a few items are ones that are required only for life to form. Most are values that are required for the *Universe, stars and planets* to form. If there were no Universe or solid matter, arguing that life could have developed differently becomes fantasy speculation.

If you want the additional variables for just *life* to form, Hugh Ross' website lists about 93 of them at www.reasons.org/fine-tuning-life-universe.

Objection 50. You are asking me to prove God does not exist. You can't prove a negative.

Response: Actually, I'm *not* asking you to prove God does not exist. I'm asking you to show me a better rational, logical and viable explanation of all the data I've shown you. You may say, "multiverses." But multiverses is the "science of the gaps," it doesn't prove anything and is un-provable and rather unrealistic and fantastical, in that it forces us to have infinite universes that cover every possible combination of choices and possibilities. Remember, too, anything you've said disparagingly about God's existence, I can say about multiverses. If you seriously believe in multiverses, you have to seriously accept the possibility of God as a fully valid alternative. I don't see many atheists willing to do that. Rather, they go around mocking the God theory and trying to suppress the information in academia.

I've provided a rational reasonable response based on

scientific data. With the multiverse idea, you've offered an un-provable speculation.

Here's an analogy. We're trying to detect who the secret spy is; I've determined seven characteristics of the spy. I say, "Agent W is Roberts from Accounting; he matches all seven characteristics – some that no one else could ever match. It's too much of a coincidence. And besides those seven characteristics, I have six more good reasons that indicate it is Roberts. Prove me wrong."

And yet you are complaining – "Oh you are trying to make me prove a negative."

No! I'm trying to say that Roberts is the man and unless you can prove my logic is wrong or my facts are wrong, you cannot disprove my argument.

If "can't prove a negative" is your only objection, then I think it fails. To refute my argument, you have to show either (a) my facts are wrong, or (b) my logic is wrong. There is simply no other way.

Besides remember I can also complain that I can't disprove the Infiniverse because I can't prove a negative, which turns the tables on you. The big difference is that I have lots of alternate facts to show God exists; you don't have any alternate facts to show the Infiniverse exists. I've provided an argument. You've not.

Objection 51. How can you say everything that begins to exist needs a cause? In your theory, God created the Universe from nothing. Therefore, the Universe had NO cause, it came from nothing.

Response: *This objection reflects a misunderstanding or ignorance of history.* Even the ancient Greeks distinguished between four "causes": the *material* cause, the *formal* cause, the *efficient* cause and the *final* cause. These are known as Aristotle's four causes. The *material cause* would be the *matter* from which the cause came, for instance in the case of the sculpture of Moses by Michelangelo, the marble was the material cause. The *formal* cause was Michelangelo's plans, his drawings. The *efficient* cause was Michelangelo himself, the actor who did the work of changing something. The *final* cause was the person for whom the statue was made (the Pope or whomever). We all agree that there was no *material* cause for the Universe. What we are arguing about here is the *efficient* cause. All science and philosophy and logic agree that there needs to be an *efficient* cause for anything that begins to exist. We have been talking about the *efficient* cause in this book. Obviously, since we agree with the Big Bang Theory, i.e., that there was a moment when the Universe began and before which there was nothing, we've aren't claiming that all matter needs a material cause. Most atheists *agree* with us that at the point of the Singularity, matter did not require a material cause. (Those who disagree will continue to hold to the theory of past infinite matter and are stuck with the infinite universe problem).

Christian Objections

Objection 52. The Big Bang is unbiblical.

Response: As a scientist with a degree in Physics, I think the Big Bang Theory may actually be one of the greatest attestations to the authenticity of Genesis. It was the bane of atheists when it was first proposed and as we've found out more, it's become even worse for what is turning out to be their blind faith beliefs.

The Big Bang is not a good name. "The Big Controlled Explosion" would be more accurate.

I once was teaching at a conference and at the end of a session, one of the attendees came up to me said he really enjoyed my presentation. Then he asked me if I liked Hugh Ross. I said I admired his work and used it a lot when witnessing to atheists. The man got angry and said, "We'll in that case I'm not coming to any more of your sessions." Later a lady came up and told me that this guy had told the group of people lining up to squeeze into my next overfilled session that I was an evolutionist. But this was a false attack by a brother in Christ. Neither I, nor Hugh Ross and Reasons to Believe, believe evolution is true. In fact his ministry has published numerous books that refute evolution specifically.

Remember the Big Bang is not equal to evolution! The Bible says the Big Bang happened; it describes something that sounds exactly like the Big Controlled Explosion. The Bible does not say evolution happened. They are two separate issues.

I think that there are valid non-compromising Christian Biblical infallible, inerrant-ist[115] theologically sound translations of Genesis that translate the word "*yom*" in Genesis 1 as day, age or eon[116] (from thinkers like Irenaeus, Basil and Thomas Aquinas etc.). As the Old Testament (Hebrew Bible) was not written in English, a truly literal translation of the Bible would refer to the original manuscripts and original languages. The argument focuses on the *translation* of the word "*yom*," not on the literal or otherwise English

---

[115] If you were wondering: I believe in the inerrancy and infallibility of Bible as written in the original languages by the original authors.

[116] This includes interpreting the curse of eating from the Tree of Knowledge of Good and Evil as being spiritual death (not physical death), i.e., separation from God which happened on the day they ate, when they were banished from the Garden and God's presence. This seems to allow physical death to exist amongst animals and plants in the eons before the fall of man.

interpretation of the word "day." But truly the argument about "*yom*" and "day" is a family argument amongst Christians. I'm not going to take a hardcore stance on either view here, but suffice it to say that I think the "old Earthists" can validly lay claim to a literal interpretation of Genesis, which includes a 13.7B year old Universe, without doing any violence to the theology, infallibility or inerrancy of the Bible as written in the original languages by the original authors. There are numerous healthy debates between Christians on this topic, and I would encourage everyone to listen to both sides of the debate and then make a rational decision.

Norm Geisler has a great article[117] titled "Does Believing In Inerrancy Require One To Believe In Young Earth Creationism?" that I recommend everyone read.

The way I see it, the Big Bang is our greatest ally in the debate about the existence of God. Genesis easily fits that scientific understanding of the Universe and helps us. See the references at the end of this book or the footnote[118] for a link to a Hebrew scholar's literal interpretation of Genesis 1 in context.

So long as we maintain the inerrancy and infallibility of the Bible, we lose nothing by understanding that the word "*yom*" could be translated differently. Again we are not talking about *interpretation* but of *translation*. For instance, "the Day of the Lord" we all understand as not being a single 24 hour day. In Genesis 2 it says, "In the *day* (*yom*) that the Lord created the heavens and the earth," yet we know that the heavens and the Earth were not created in a day. Therefore, we realize that the word "day" located in the very the same narrative, can rationally and logically and without compromise be translated as "period of time."

For an additional resource, please refer to Hugh Ross's *A Matter of Days: Resolving a Creation Controversy,* NavPress Publishing Group, 1st edition (June 1, 2004).

As far as atheists are concerned, once we prove God exists, we can then argue about if the Bible is accurate. But we'll keep that as a separate issue (and it will be addressed in an upcoming book in this No Blind Faith series).

I always advise my friends to not get hung up on the 6 days vs. 6 eons when they talk to atheists (though it's a fun debate

---

[117] http://normangeisler.net/articles/Bible/Inspiration-Inerrancy/DoesInerrancyRequireBeliefInYoungEarth.pdf

[118] www.CreationInGenesis.com

amongst us Christians). Though I have given many sermons refuting evolution, I also tell folks, don't get stuck with trying to disprove evolution because I've found that it's far too much work and every week there's a new article that I have to become an expert on. With the Agent X argument, we are using logic to come to a conclusion. Logic doesn't change! We can prove scientifically, logically, and rationally that there must be a Creator. Evolution deals with biology on Earth; it does not deal with the existence of the Creator. Once we agree on the existence of the Creator, then the methods of His creating man is just a matter of methodology.

I also don't **start** a conversation with atheists by trying to prove the Bible is accurate; I save that for *after* I've gotten them to agree that it's reasonable for a God to exist. They may not believe it, but once they are willing to agree that it's a reasonable option, I'm ready to then move to Step 2, i.e., proving the Bible is accurate.

So you first want to prove that God exists. It is easier to do that when you start by using data the atheist *already* accepts, like the Big Bang Theory.

Objection 53. Are we changing our interpretation of the Bible to fit science?

Response: I don't think so - actually it seems like science is changing to fit us. For example, Augustine said that we cannot conceive of what kind of day it was[119] and many other ancients said the word *yom* could be *translated* (not interpreted) as *eon*, not *day*.[120]

And we can't claim they were interpreting the Bible to fit science, since science didn't know about the Big Bang Theory or the age of the Earth till the 20th Century. Augustine even claimed that Time had a beginning (in that same chapter). A concept that science rejected till the Big Bang was discovered.

It looks like science finally came around to agreeing with Christianity, not vice versa.

---

[119] St. Augustine, *City of God (1467)*, Henry Bettenson (transl) (London: Penguin Books, 1972), Book 11, chap. 6.
[120] Find out both sides at: www.GenevanInstitute.org/syllabus/unit-two-theology-proper/lesson-5-the-decree-of-creation/pca-creation-committee-report/

Objection 54. You can't and shouldn't try to prove God exists. It has to be believed on faith. If you knew that God existed, then it wouldn't be faith.

Response: Actually, this is not a Biblical viewpoint. As we show in one of the books in this series, titled *No Blind Faith*, blind faith is sinful and unbiblical. Repeatedly the Old Testament tells how God punishes those who have blind faith. He essentially says to them, "I brought you out of the land of Egypt, I parted the Red Sea, I fed you in the wilderness, I did all these things proving I was God, and yet you go into the market, buy a piece of wood, cook with part of it and pray to the other part of it. You blindly believe that it is a god despite the fact that it has never done anything to prove itself like I have. For that you are evil." Then God punishes them severely by sending in their enemies to conquer them.[121] Even Jesus proved He was God repeatedly, as when He healed the paralytic and said, "Anyone can say your sins are forgiven, but to prove to you that I can actually forgive sins, I say 'rise up and walk.'"[122]

Finally, notice who are named in the Faith Hall of Fame according to the New Testament: Moses, Abraham, and Enoch. These were men who had personally seen God and knew He existed.[123] They didn't have blind faith, they had 100% proof that God existed and yet they are considered the men of the greatest faith. Too often in Christianity we have misused the word "faith." To understand what the word faith meant in Christ's time, substitute the word "trust." The meanings underlying "faith" and "trust" are not so much nouns as they are *action verbs*. You believe and act.

For more information on faith and blind faith please go to www.NoBlindFaith.com/sermon/sermons.htm and click on "Mythbusters: Blind Faith."

---

[121] *See*, e.g., Ezekiel 20:10; Isaiah 44:15-19; Jeremiah 2 &10:1-5.

[122] *See* Mark 2:1-8.

[123] *See* Hebrews 11:1-40.

Appendix II:
Some of the Fine Tuning Parameters for The Universe

There are many known parameters that have to be fine-tuned or the Universe and/or life would not exist. These parameters are referenced in Cosmologist Hugh Ross's book, *The Creator and the Cosmos.*[124] Ross says that we are discovering new parameters on a regular basis. Ross lists about 93 on their webpage: www.reasons.org/fine-tuning-life-universe. I've selected what I consider the 37 least contentious ones and listed them.

I've also split up the parameters into two groups. Group One includes the parameters that are required for the Universe to exist and for *any* sort of life to exist. Group Two are the parameters that are required for *human or organic life* to exist. Note that an atheist cannot claim an anthropomorphological bias for the first group.

Group One
1. **ratio of electromagnetic force to gravity** *if larger:* all stars would be at least 40% more massive than the sun; hence, stellar burning would be too brief and too uneven for life support; *if smaller:* all stars would be at least 20% less massive than the sun, thus incapable of producing heavy elements.
2. **expansion rate of universe** *if larger:* no galaxy formation; *if smaller:* universe would have collapsed prior to star formation.
3. **mass of universe** *if larger:* overabundance of deuterium from Big Bang would cause stars to burn rapidly, too rapidly for life to form; *if smaller:* insufficient helium from Big Bang would result in a shortage of heavy elements.
4. **cosmological constant** *if larger:* universe would expand too quickly to form solar-type stars; *if smaller:* stars would remain so cool that nuclear fusion would never ignite, hence no heavy element
5. **ratio of electromagnetic force constant to gravitational force constant** *if larger:* all stars would be at least 40% more massive than the sun; hence, stellar burning would be too brief and too uneven for

---

124 Published by NavPress Publishing Group (1995).

life support; *if smaller:* all stars would be at least 20% less massive than the sun, thus incapable of producing heavy elements.

6. **ratio of number of protons to number of electrons** *if larger:* electromagnetism would dominate gravity, preventing galaxy, star, and planet formation; *if smaller:* same as above.

7. **entropy level of the Universe** *if larger:* stars would not form within proto-galaxies; *if smaller:* no proto-galaxies would form.

8. **mass density of the Universe** *if larger:* overabundance of deuterium from Big Bang would cause stars to burn rapidly, too rapidly for any sort of life to form; *if smaller:* insufficient helium from Big Bang would result in a shortage of heavy elements.

9. **initial uniformity of radiation** *if more uniform:* stars, star clusters, and galaxies would not have formed; *if less uniform:* universe by now would be mostly black holes and empty space.

10. **average distance between galaxies** *if larger:* star formation late enough in the history of the Universe would be hampered by lack of material; *if smaller:* gravitational tug-of-wars would destabilize the sun's orbit.

11. **density of galaxy cluster** *if denser:* galaxy collisions and mergers would disrupt the sun's orbit; *if less dense:* star formation late enough in the history of the Universe would be hampered by lack of material.

12. **fine structure constant** (describing the fine-structure splitting of spectral lines); *if larger:* all stars would be at least 30% less massive than the sun; *if larger* than 0.06: matter would be unstable in large magnetic fields; *if smaller:* all stars would be at least 80% more massive than the sun.

13. **initial excess of nucleons over anti-nucleons** *if greater:* radiation would prohibit planet formation; *if lesser:* matter would be insufficient for galaxy or star formation.

14. **ratio of exotic matter mass to ordinary matter mass** *if larger:* universe would collapse before solar-type stars could form; *if smaller:* no galaxies would form.

15. **number of effective dimensions in the early universe** *if larger:* quantum mechanics, gravity, and relativity could not coexist; thus **any** life would be impossible; *if smaller:* same result.

16. **number of effective dimensions in the present universe** *if smaller:* electron, planet, and star orbits would become unstable; *if larger:* same result.

17. **mass of the neutrino** *if smaller:* galaxy clusters, galaxies, and stars would not form; *if larger:* galaxy clusters and galaxies would be too

dense.

18. Big Bang ripples *if smaller:* galaxies would not form; universe would expand too rapidly; *if larger:* galaxies/galaxy clusters would be too dense for life; black holes would dominate; universe would collapse before life-site could form.

Group Two

19. size of the relativistic dilation factor *if smaller:* certain life-essential chemical reactions will not function properly; *if larger:* same result.

20. uncertainty magnitude in the Heisenberg uncertainty principle *if smaller:* oxygen transport to body cells would be too small and certain life-essential elements would be unstable; *if larger:* oxygen transport to body cells would be too great and certain life-essential elements would be unstable.

21. ^{12}C to ^{16}O nuclear energy level ratio *if larger:* universe would contain insufficient oxygen for life; *if smaller:* universe would contain insufficient carbon for life.

22. ground state energy level for ^4He *if larger:* universe would contain insufficient carbon and oxygen for life; *if smaller:* same as above.

23. decay rate of ^8Be *if slower:* heavy element fusion would generate catastrophic explosions in all the stars; *if faster:* no element heavier than beryllium would form; thus, no life chemistry.

24. white dwarf binaries *if too few:* insufficient fluorine would exist for life chemistry; *if too many:* planetary orbits would be too unstable for life; *if formed too soon:* insufficient fluorine production; *if formed too late:* fluorine would arrive too late for life chemistry.

25. strong nuclear force constant *if larger:* no hydrogen would form; atomic nuclei for most life-essential elements would be unstable; thus, no life chemistry; *if smaller:* no elements heavier than hydrogen would form: again, no life chemistry.

26. weak nuclear force constant *if larger:* too much hydrogen would convert to helium in Big Bang; hence, stars would convert too much matter into heavy elements making life chemistry impossible; *if smaller:* too little helium would be produced from Big Bang; hence, stars would convert too little matter into heavy elements making life chemistry impossible.

27. gravitational force constant *if larger:* stars would be too hot and would burn too rapidly and too unevenly for life chemistry; *if smaller:* stars would be too cool to ignite nuclear fusion; thus, many of the elements needed for life chemistry would never form.

28. **electromagnetic force constant** *if greater:* chemical bonding would be disrupted; elements more massive than boron would be unstable to fission; *if lesser:* chemical bonding would be insufficient for life chemistry.

29. **ratio of electrons to protons** *if larger or smaller:* chemical bonding would be insufficient for life chemistry.

30. **ratio of electron to proton *mass*** *if larger or smaller:* chemical bonding would be insufficient for life chemistry.

31. **velocity of light** *if faster:* stars would be too luminous for life support; *if slower:* stars would be insufficiently luminous for life support.

32. **age of the Universe** *if older:* no solar-type stars in a stable burning phase would exist in the right (for life) part of the galaxy; *if younger:* solar-type stars in a stable burning phase would not yet have formed.

33. **average distance between stars** *if larger:* heavy element density would be too sparse for rocky planets to form; *if smaller:* planetary orbits would be too unstable for life.

34. **decay rate of protons** *if greater:* life would be exterminated by the release of radiation; *if smaller:* universe would contain insufficient matter for life.

35. **ratio of neutron mass to proton mass** *if higher:* neutron decay would yield too few neutrons for the formation of many life-essential elements; *if lower:* neutron decay would produce so many neutrons as to collapse all stars into neutron stars or black holes.

36. **polarity of the water molecule** *if greater:* heat of fusion and vaporization would be too high for life; *if smaller:* heat of fusion and vaporization would be too low for life; liquid water would not work as a solvent for life chemistry; ice would not float, and a runaway freeze-up would result.

37. **supernovae eruptions** *if too close, too frequent, or too late:* radiation would exterminate life on the planet; *if too distant, too infrequent, or too soon:* heavy elements would be too sparse for rocky planets to form.

Neil Mammen

Appendix III:
Using This Information Without Fear

Okay, you have all this great information, but you are both not sure you understand all the technical details *and* not sure how to engage with someone about this.

As we mentioned in the introduction, we at No Blind Faith want to train you to easily and fearlessly use this information to engage with your friends and coworkers.

So, to enable you to talk to your friends and co-workers we recommend the following:

1. First and foremost, do not launch into a witnessing "take no prisoners spree." Instead, we recommend you use the techniques that Gregory Koukl and the STR team suggest in the "Columbo Tactic." To learn about this excellent tactic (which we did not invent but have shamelessly stolen to use ourselves), we recommend you go to the STR website (www.str.org), or use this link through our website **www.NoBlindFaith.com/Columbo.htm**.

   We would replicate the tactic here, but we would not have done as good a job as Gregory,[125] and I imagine it would violate some copyrights.

   In his write-up of this tactic, Gregory explains how to gently ask questions and engage with others such that you are piquing their interest and asking probing but non-confrontational questions. Gregory expands on this in his CD and DVD series, "Tactics in Defending the Faith" and his book, *Tactics: A Game Plan for Discussing Your Christian Convictions*.

   All are available at the STR website www.str.org. We highly recommend this resource.

2. Let's focus specifically on how to use the information that you've *just* read in this book. My favorite way to do this is to

---

[125] Yes, I know, we all call him Greg when we hang out with him, but he's officially "Gregory."

say to anyone at work or wherever: "I just read a book that talks about how the Big Bang may indicate that you need a first cause that is outside of time and space and must be personal. Have you read anything about this? What do you think about that?"

Or I ask, "Did you know: recent research indicates there are more than 4 dimensions, which may indicate that the concept of beings that can intersect our dimension may actually have a scientific basis. Isn't that interesting? Have you ever thought about that?"

If they show an interest, ask them more questions. You can then start to engage with them, feeding a few things here and there. Maybe you can give them a copy of this book and ask them to evaluate it.

3. When you introduce this material to them or give them this book, do not need to feel you "own" the material. Let it stand and fall on its own merits. What we mean by that is: you should not feel that you have to defend every point or concept of this book. After all, we may be wrong, too. So if your friends disagree with anything, ask them to explain why they disagree. See if their disagreement is valid, yet do not feel like you have to defend us, or confront them or convince them of its validity. However, it's important that you understand what their objections are and see if you can resolve them for yourself. Feel free to ask them questions to clarify, then go research it. When you've done the research, you can get back to them and say: "This is what my research yielded," and present it to them. You are first their friend. But if in doing so you find we are wrong, send us an email. We need to correct it. Or have *them* email me at neil_agentX@noblindfaith.com.

4. I always try to say this when I talk to other folks about anything religious or philosophical: "This is what I found to be important personally, you may or may not approach it the same way. If it's of value, that's great. If not, then just ignore it completely." For one, it's true and secondly, it's what they are going to do anyway.

5. An approach to arguments about politics, religion and the like, advocated by author and talk-show host Dennis Prager,

is to explain to the other person that you value *clarity* over *agreement*. You can advance the cause of truth by helping the other person see what exactly he or she believes, and how it contrasts with your beliefs. This approach allows both people to explore ideas and see where they lead, while not making the conversation all about who has "scored a point" or "won." In this way, the approach keeps the conversation cooler, more interesting, less defensive, and more likely to keep a friend.

6. You will make mistakes and after any such encounter, you will remember 10 things you should have said or a better way to have responded. That's fine. That's how you learn. During a recent sermon, I recounted how I'd responded to a skeptic (actually someone who worked for Americans United for Separation of Church and State, an atheist organization) in such a way that this skeptic said, "Hmm, I've never thought about that."

   After my talk, a gentleman came up to me and said, "How do I get there? How do I learn what to say to skeptics?"

   I responded, "Actually you only heard the successful encounter, you haven't heard about the 50 times before that, with other skeptics where I walked away and then later said: 'Rats, if only I'd said this other thing instead.'"

   The point is that you learn by experience. After every encounter, you'll think of things and ways to respond that is more loving, more coherent, and easier to understand. That's how you get there. Remember those times and those lessons and look for more opportunities. I guarantee they'll come. This time you'll be ready. Just keep doing it with love.

Never forget the third leg of the No Blind Faith motto: *Relationship*. You can't change minds easily unless you win their respect and they know you care.

So go get them.

Appendix IV:
References and Research Sources

Here are some great websites and resources for more reading and additional information.

1. William Lane Craig, Reasonable Faith: www.WilliamLaneCraig.com
Craig always wins public debates with atheists. See especially the Kalam Cosmological Argument and his Q&A section.

2. Gregory Koukl, Stand to Reason: www.STR.org
Gregory is a master at tactics for defending the faith and rational thought.

3. Hugh Ross, Reasons to Believe: www.Reasons.org
Hugh is an astrophysicist and can provide much of the scientific research you need.

4. Frank Turek, Cross Examined: www.CrossExamined.org
Frank is the co-author of *I don't have enough Faith to be an Atheist*, (Crossway Books, 2004). A book I highly recommend everyone own and reread every few years.

5. Dr. Rodney Whitefield: www.CreationInGenesis.com
Dr. Whitefield is a Hebrew scholar who believes in the inerrancy and infallibility of the Bible. His careful scholarly analysis in figuring out the day/age issue in Genesis can be found at his website. It is useful as part of your research into this issue.

6. iPod/MP3 Downloads: I heartily encourage you to download these
mp3 debates and talks from over 20 different speakers and listen to them during your commute or exercise.
www.NoBlindFaith.com/Sermon/ApologeticsResources.htm

Neil Mammen

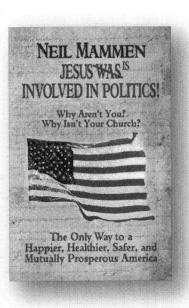

How often have you been told:
"Jesus wasn't involved in Politics,"
"Jesus was a Socialist,"
"You can't legislate Morality,"
"Laws don't change hearts,"
"The Church should stick to preaching the Gospel"?

Wish you had a Biblical and Logical way to show your pastor and friends that these are all FALSE?

Weary of trying to get your pastor or congregation to speak out against laws that are destroying the USA? Fearful for your children's religious freedoms?

This is your reference manual!
Show that if Christians voted biblically; within a few election cycles, poverty would be reduced, welfare would be needed less, taxes would be cut, crime would go down, families would start to mend and all Americans would be free and prosper.
Learn why even atheists should want Christian lawmakers.

Let's get churches involved and encourage pastors to teach our churches how God's law protects the innocent, the poor, the widows and orphans.
Learn why *not* being involved in politics violates the second greatest commandment!
Used correctly these arguments can change pastors' minds and awaken The Sleeping Giant of the American Church.

"One third apologetics, one third theology, one third politics, all relevant. This book explains a lot of what you see in the world today."

Start a Book Club or Bible Study with this book.
www.JesusIsInvolvedInPolitics.com

References for Neil Mammen

If you are looking for someone who teaches apologetics and doesn't apologize for it, Neil's the guy you want to call. I recommend his teaching highly and so do the people of our church. He is witty, funny, engaging, insightful, deep, easy to listen to, hard to ignore.
Bill Buchholz, Senior Pastor, Family Community Church

Neil's messages not only reflect professional and Scriptural integrity, but his sense of humor adds the well-rounded touch that keeps our congregation anticipating his next visit or series.
David Underwood, Senior Pastor, Liberty Ridge Church

Neil has a gift that spans all age groups. This is because I can name none that exceeds Neil's preparedness when he takes the pulpit. Neil has sound Doctrine and Theology. His style is relevant yet it remains biblically sound. You can expect dynamic visuals and creatively enhanced teaching that pulls each hearer in!
Chuck Aruta, Senior Pastor, New Beginnings Church

Neil is both dynamic and exciting to listen to. He is able to captivate an audience of any age from Jr. High to adults! Neil has a unique ability to take deep and sometimes complicated spiritual truths and communicates them in a relevant way. He speaks both to the mind and the heart. Not only can I speak to his ability as a speaker, I can also speak of his character (and his love of gadgets). Neil lives his life with integrity and his love for God is evident. He is generous, hospitable and faithful, both in his relationships with people as well as with God.
Adam Miller, Senior Pastor, Ceres Christian Church

I love Neil's passion to communicate truths that matter. Whether he is speaking of the rationality of the Christian worldview, or the mandate for Christians to engage culture with a broad and winsome presence in all fields and vocations, whether speaking to students or adults, his thought is clear, his presentation entertaining and compelling, and his authentic and whole-hearted commitment obvious to all who interact with his prophetic message.
Jeff Reed, Senior Pastor, Hillside Covenant Church

www.NoBlindFaith.com

Neil Mammen can be scheduled to speak on this and other topics at churches, retreats, classes, seminars, groups, schools, and youth events anywhere in the world. Honorariums are at each group's discretion.

Neil is a Corporate Motivational Speaker weaving in motivational biblical principles in a non-offensive non-confrontational, rational, and logical way for a secular audience. **Contact info: Speaking@NoBlindFaith.com**

No Blind Faith is happy to make slides and notes available for teaching this content to Sunday Schools, Bible Studies, and Churches. An Agent X study guide targeted at Junior High to the Adult levels will be available soon. For information, contact us.

Hand this book out to your friends! Quantity copies are available at deep discounts. CD's and DVDs of this in sermon form are also available.

For information: **AgentX@NoBlindFaith.com**

Be proud of your Rational Faith!
**Badges, Stickers, Polos and T-Shirts with the No Blind Faith Logo
are available at www.NoBlindFaith.com and at www.J3IP.com**

Made in the USA
Middletown, DE
22 September 2016